PRAISE FOR
MAKING THE CASE FOR CHRISTIANITY

Making the Case for Christianity is a carefully reasoned and clearly written defense of some of the central truth-claims of historic Christianity. This collection of helpful and timely apologetics essays responds specifically to some of the popular and controversial claims made by various current critics of Christianity. This volume testifies well to the truth that historic Christianity is a faith that involves knowledge and is indeed compatible with reason.

—Kenneth Samples
Senior Research Scholar at Reasons to Believe
Author of *7 Truths That Changed the World* (Baker, 2012)

This book is a brilliant compilation of fresh articles addressing and answering the major, current objections the devote Christian is forced to address or give in to a murky and intellectually suicidal faith. A murky faith is one that is not critically examined at all, and believed blindly, and an intellectually suicidal faith is one that cannot stand the test of critical objections and inquiry when put to the test. This book demolishes both of these theses. This is an exceptional book that I enthusiastically endorse.

—Khaldoun A. Sweis, PhD
Chair and Assistant Professor of Philosophy
Olive-Harvey College in Chicago
Editor of *Christian Apologetics: An Anthology of Primary Sources* (Zondervan, 2012) and *Debating Christian Theism* (Oxford, 2013)

This book is distinctively Lutheran, patently Christian, and genuinely winsome. As such, believers from all branches of Christendom will find this volume both attractive and beneficial. Although the chapters in this fine text focus on a range of topics and are written by different contributors, their commonality is this: every page of this book communicates the Gospel and exalts Jesus. Indeed, such a Christocentric methodology is the best way to make the case for Christianity.

—David W. Jones, PhD
Associate Professor of Christian Ethics
Southeastern Baptist Theological Seminary
Wake Forest, North Carolina

Not a primer nor an encyclopedia, here is the mid-range apologetics we have needed. The authors address several recent challenges to the Christian account of life with responses that are sometimes contentious, sometimes sympathetic, always insightful, and ultimately constructive—a defense that is not merely defensive. The reader will find timely and useable discussions about current apologetics issues that matter.

—Russ Moulds, PhD
Professor of Psychology and Education
Concordia University Nebraska
Editor and author of *A Teacher of the Church* (Wipf & Stock, 2007)

Making the Case for Christianity is a page turner, with plenty to reward both budding and seasoned apologists. I've worked on and around these issues for decades, but I found myself repeatedly underlining and circling new things to incorporate into upcoming talks.

And the citations are a treasure. Where I found myself taking a different tack with my answers, I still appreciated their pointed and clear-spoken observations.

—Mark Coppenger, PhD
Professor of Christian Apologetics
The Southern Baptist Theological Seminary
Louisville, Kentucky

MAKING THE CASE FOR CHRISTIANITY

MAKING THE CASE FOR CHRISTIANITY

RESPONDING TO MODERN OBJECTIONS

EDITED BY KOREY D. MAAS
AND ADAM S. FRANCISCO

Peer Reviewed

CONCORDIA PUBLISHING HOUSE · SAINT LOUIS

Peer Reviewed

Copyright © 2014 Concordia Publishing House
3558 S. Jefferson Ave., St. Louis, MO 63118–3968
1-800-325-3040 • www.cph.org

Manufactured in the United States of America

Library of Congress Cataloging-in-Publication Data

Making the case for Christianity : responding to modern objections / edited by Korey D. Maas and Adam S. Francisco.

  pages cm

Includes index.

ISBN 978-0-7586-4419-0

1. Apologetics. I. Maas, Korey. II. Francisco, Adam.

BT1105.M26 2014

239--dc23   2013033439

1 2 3 4 5 6 7 8 9 10   23 22 21 20 19 18 17 16 15 14

CONTENTS

FOREWORD

The word *apologetics* comes from the Greek word for "defense." Christian apologetics is not necessarily about trying to argue someone into the faith, if that were possible. At its heart, apologetics is about defending Christianity from those who attack it. Today Christianity is being attacked from so many different sides, tarnished with so many false charges, and obscured with so many misconceptions that the apologetics enterprise—that is, defending the faith—is critically important. The attacks need to be fended off, the charges answered, and the misconceptions cleared up so that Christianity can at least gain a hearing, which is all the Word of God needs to create faith (Romans 10:17).

G. K. Chesterton has described how Christianity is "attacked on all sides and for all contradictory reasons."[1] Some criticize Christianity for its gentleness; some for provoking so many wars. Some think Christianity is too optimistic; others that it is too pessimistic. Some attack it for its gloom and others for its joy. Sometimes, such contradictory criticisms can be found in a single tract or conversation. Chesterton wrote,

> What again could this astonishing thing be like which people were so anxious to contradict, that in doing so they did not mind contradicting themselves? . . . If this mass of mad contradictions really existed, quakerish and bloodthirsty, too gorgeous and too thread-bare, austere, yet pandering

---

[1] G. K. Chesterton, "The Paradoxes of Christianity," *Orthodoxy*, in *The Everyman Chesterton*, ed. Ian Ker (New York: Everyman's Library, 2011), 333.

preposterously to the lust of the eye, the enemy of women and their foolish refuge, a solemn pessimist and a silly optimist, if this evil existed, then there was in this evil something quite supreme and unique. . . . And then in a quiet hour a strange thought struck me like a still thunderbolt. There had suddenly come into my mind another explanation. Suppose we heard an unknown man spoken of by many men. Suppose we were puzzled to hear that some men said he was too tall and some too short; some objected to his fatness, some lamented his leanness; some thought him too dark, and some too fair. One explanation (as has been already admitted) would be that he might be an odd shape. But there is another explanation. He might be the right shape.[2]

Today Christianity is being attacked for being too rational and for being too emotional, for its moral strictness and for its immorality, for being unscientific and for claiming to be true. Modernists dismiss Christianity for its subjectivity; Postmodernists dismiss Christianity for its objectivity.

This book is a collection of essays that defend Christianity from the various charges against it that are being made today. Many of them come down to cases of circular reasoning in which underlying tacit assumptions (e.g., the material world is all there is) determine the conclusions (anything miraculous cannot be real). Others assert as facts statements that just are not true (such as Christianity being responsible for war, slavery, and genocide). Some of the reasons given today for rejecting Christianity are philosophical (God's existence violates science or is disproven because of the problem of evil). Others are moral (Christianity is unfair; God allows evil; the Christian cultural legacy is immoral). Others are existential (Christianity cannot be "the only truth" in a culture of religious pluralism). These essays give good reasons for thinking otherwise.

Joshua Pagán explains a variation of the cosmological argument for the existence of God ("All things that exist have a cause. . . .") that

---

[2] Chesterton, "The Paradoxes of Christianity," *Orthodoxy*, 337–39.

is adapted to the findings of contemporary science. The "Kalam Cosmological Argument" begins, "all things that *begin to* exist have a cause." Old-fashioned materialists insisted that the universe has always existed and so denied that it needed a cause. But now, nearly all scientists accept the evidence for the Big Bang theory, which means that the universe did, in fact, "begin to exist." Since the universe had a beginning, it must have a cause, and that cause must be outside the universe. That cause must be a necessary being, something—or Someone—without a cause; that is to say, God. Thus, contemporary science makes a classic argument for God's existence credible again.

The "Kalam" argument is a contribution of medieval Islam. Challenges to Christianity today come not only from atheists but also from believers in other religions. Adam Francisco takes on Islam's critique of the deity of Christ. John Bombaro deals with the challenge of religious pluralism—how Christianity can claim to offer the only means of salvation in light of the multitude of world religions.

Ironically, challenges to Christianity also come from ostensibly Christian scholarship. A common theme throughout these essays is the influence of the historical critical approach to Scripture. That the Bible is not historically accurate, that the supernatural events recorded in the Gospels are embellishments of an oral tradition, and that the historical Jesus evolved into the Christ of faith as a construction of the church are notions taken for granted in mainstream biblical scholarship and are widely taught in Christian seminaries. This book shows how the historical critical approach to the Bible as developed by liberal theologians is being used both by the "new atheists" and by contemporary Muslims to attack the teachings of Christianity.

In this book, Mark Pierson and Craig Parton offer spirited defenses of the historical reliability of the Gospels and the central fact they record: the resurrection of Jesus Christ. This view of Scripture is also supported by Dr. Bombaro, who cites the observation that the message of the Gospel is not "good ideas" or "good advice," but "good news."

Korey Maas addresses the "new atheists'" contention that Christianity is the source of slavery, war, genocide, oppression, and virtually every other social evil. These charges are not only grotesque slanders, as almost every historian would agree, but the fact is that Christianity also actively countered these evils. Dr. Maas shows how Church Fathers such as Augustine, Cyprian, Clement, and Gregory of Nyssa opposed slavery, as did the medieval popes. The defenders of slavery did so on the authority of Aristotle, and race-based slavery was largely a product of the Enlightenment, with Voltaire, Hobbes, and Locke defending the practice. Those who crusaded for the abolition of slavery, on the other hand, were nearly always Christians motivated by their faith. Dr. Maas agrees that Christians have been complicit in sinful practices in a fallen world—after all, Christianity is about sin and its forgiveness, not creating a utopia—but it is absurd to deny that Christianity has been an influence for good.

Angus Menuge addresses what may be the most challenging argument from non-believers—the question of how a good, all-powerful, and omniscient God could allow so much evil and suffering in the world. Dr. Menuge gives a lucid survey of the issue in its different forms and in the different answers that Christian thinkers have given to the problem. But then he does something more profound. He distinguishes between "philosophical theism," in which God is imagined as an abstract, transcendent collection of qualities who looks down from above on a suffering world, and Jesus Christ, God incarnate and crucified. The Christian belief that God in Christ bore in his body the sins, the sufferings, the afflictions, and the evils of the world to redeem that world transforms the whole question.

This is a distinctly Lutheran apologetic. Dr. Menuge is employing Luther's distinction between the "theology of glory," which seeks glib answers and confident understanding, and the "theology of the cross," which finds God in weakness and suffering. Our trials force us to depend not on ourselves but on Christ, who bears our burdens. Dr. Menuge concludes, "*Christ* is God's answer to the problem of evil." And in his resurrection—again, the fact of the empty tomb—we can find God's triumph over evil and hope for our lives.

The other essays, too, while making the case for Christianity in general, are distinctly Lutheran in their approach. Instead of speculating about God as a philosophical principle, the authors do as Luther recommends, bringing the discussion to God incarnate, to the very tangible Jesus Christ.

> Therefore whenever you consider the doctrine of justification and wonder how or where or in what condition to find a God who justifies or accepts sinners, then you must know that there is no other God than this Man Jesus Christ. Take hold of Him; cling to Him with all your heart, and spurn all speculation about the Divine Majesty; for whoever investigates the majesty of God will be consumed by His glory. I know from experience what I am talking about. . . . Christ Himself says: "I am the Way, and the Truth, and the Life; no one comes to the Father, but by Me" (John 14:6). Outside Christ, the Way, therefore, you will find no other way to the Father; you will find only wandering, not truth, but hypocrisy and lies, not life, but eternal death. Take note, therefore, in the doctrine of justification or grace that when we all must struggle with the Law, sin, death, and the devil, we must look at no other God than this incarnate and human God.[3]

Thus, every essay keeps coming back to the concrete, historic, tangible fact of Christ and the proof of his identity in the objective reality of the empty tomb. This approach to apologetics—which derives from the great apologist John Warwick Montgomery (cited throughout these essays), a Missouri Synod Lutheran—is in accord with the Lutheran emphasis on objectivity. (For example, justification is not merely a subjective experience nor an intellectual conclusion, but an objective work of God.) Lutheran theology also emphasizes the realm of the physical and the material (in the incarnation, in the cross in which Jesus bore the sin of the world, and in the Sacraments, in

---

[3] Martin Luther, *Lectures on Galatians: Chapters 1–4*, trans. Jaroslav Pelikan, *Luther's Works* (St. Louis: Concordia, 1963) 26:29.

which the saving grace of God is conveyed through water, bread, and wine). As Dr. Bombaro puts it here, "with the incarnation the eternal touches time, supernatural becomes natural, the metaphysical dons physicality, the unseen is seen, grace invades nature."

The other characteristically Lutheran emphasis in these essays is the emphasis on the Gospel. Craig Parton's legal argument for the Resurrection culminates in a proclamation of what the Resurrection means: "In Jesus Christ we find the announcement that, though we have brought about our own doom by our cosmic rebellion against God, God himself has acted to effect a reconciliation wholly incapable of being effected by sinful man."

Believers as well as non-believers can benefit from Christian apologetics, which builds the conviction that the teachings of the Christian faith—the triune God, the cross, salvation, everlasting life—are not just good ideas or comforting teachings; rather, they are objectively, actually *true*.

GENE EDWARD VEITH

INTRODUCTION

Korey D. Maas

Our twenty-first century is increasingly described as part of a new "post-Christian" era in western civilization. Long gone is the millennium and more of Christendom, during which the Christian religion infused and informed—often in an official capacity—virtually every aspect of western life and thought. Also fading away is the less cooperative yet still accommodating modern era ushered in with the Enlightenment, which, while refusing officially to sanction any uniquely Christian truth claims or any ecclesiastical role in the public ordering of society, continued to allow for significant Christian influence by virtue of the simple fact that the individual inhabitants of the western world continued in the main to profess Christianity.

Demographic and ideological shifts, however, continue to alter the religious landscape of a twenty-first century characterized by developments such as globalism and its accompanying pluralism. Twentieth-century inventions such as the internet and satellite television have brought, and continue to bring, us continually closer to geographically distant people and theologically distant ideas than was the case even a century ago. The ease of international travel made possible by the airplane further allows us not only to know much more *about* peoples with very different lifestyles and beliefs, but to know these people themselves. Thus even the smallest American cities can increasingly be described as cosmopolitan—world cities which reflect the pluralistic cacophony of competing religions, philosophies, and lifestyles present in the wider world itself.

Acknowledging with the Preacher of Ecclesiastes, though, that there is "nothing new under the sun" (Ecclesiastes 1:9), one might note that the contours of this post-Christian era are not, strictly speaking, new at all. Indeed, they look increasingly like those of the pre-Christian era of the Early Church, those centuries before the conversion of the Roman Emperor Constantine and the eventual elevation of Christianity to the privileged status of "official" religion of the Roman Empire and, subsequently, the western world. The Christian religion was born into, and rose to prominence within, a cultural milieu no less pluralistic than our own. The apostles and their successors in the centuries immediately following proclaimed the Gospel throughout an Empire bustling with an officially tolerated Judaism, imperially sanctioned Greco-Roman cults, mystery religions imported from the East, and various local, tribal, and familial pieties. They were further confronted with philosophies such as Platonism, Stoicism, and Epicureanism, each with its own religious connotations and expressions.

Given this pluralistic context, combined with Christianity's status both as a minority faith and a suspiciously "novel" religion, it is perhaps not surprising that the century following the death of the last apostle would come to be known as the golden age of Christian apologetics, of intellectual defenses of the Christian faith made to those—Greek philosophers, Roman emperors, adherents of Judaism and the multiple other religions of antiquity—either skeptical of or hostile to the unique tenets of Christianity.[1] Though the prerogatives of post-apostolic Christians certainly need not be deemed normative for the contemporary church, it is nevertheless suggestive that the Early Church, encountering a religious and philosophical pluralism very much like our own, felt compelled to formulate and to present defenses of the faith to those who would reject and even persecute it. Further suggesting that a similar apologetic thrust might be especially valuable today is not only the similarity between Christianity's first centuries and the twenty-first, but also one very notable difference.

---

[1] See, e.g., Robert M. Grant, *Greek Apologists of the Second Century* (Philadelphia: Westminster Press, 1988).

While the Christianity of the first three centuries, as today, found itself continually in competition with a variety of alternative religions, it did not face anything like the popular atheism, or even anti-theism, present in our own day. While the debates of antiquity swirled around the question of which particular religion was true, the atheism prominent since the nineteenth century—and more than usually vocal in our own generation—brings a strident new voice to the debate, one which dismisses all religious belief as fundamentally irrational.

Being cognizant of the intellectual and cultural context in which the church now finds itself, a pluralistic context in which antipathy to Christianity is ever more common, the Christian remains well advised to be "prepared to make a defense [*apologia*] to anyone who asks you for a reason for the hope that is in you" (1 Peter 3:15). To the extent, however, that "making a defense" might involve "having an argument"—even if conducted, as the apostle exhorts, with gentleness and respect—some object to apologetic endeavors by pronouncing that one cannot "argue people into faith." This is indeed true; but it is also beside the point since the apologist neither presumes nor proposes to argue people into faith. The defense of Christianity is a defense of that religion which proclaims unambiguously in its Scriptures that saving faith is a gift of the Holy Spirit at work in the proclamation of the Gospel (1 Corinthians 12:3; Romans 10:17).

And yet faith is never without an object; it remains always faith in something, or, more specifically, someone. Therefore, Christian apologetics primarily addresses itself to those objections—explicit, implicit, or assumed—which the non-Christian embraces in his or her attempts to justify a dismissal of the Gospel's content. Unsurprisingly, these objections are most frequently aimed at matters of fact, at those Christian claims which might at least in theory be verified or falsified either by some deductive logical means or by some inductive empirical means. The proclamation to unbelievers that their sins are forgiven on account of God becoming man, dying and rising again, might of course meet objections on any number of levels. The unbeliever might object that he does not even believe God exists, so any talk of God becoming man is superfluous. She might accept that there is a God, but reject that Jesus was in fact God, ever claimed to be God, or perhaps even ever existed. He might object that Jesus, if he did exist, did not and could not have risen from death. But the objection will almost certainly not be: "Yes, I believe that God exists, that he was incarnate in Christ, and that Christ did actually die and rise again; I just don't believe that my sins are forgiven as a result." In other words, the non-Christian's objections are not to "things unseen," such as the removal of sin, but to those truth claims which are at least in principle open to logical or empirical evaluation.

That the Christian faith even allows for such investigation of its central claims is one of the features that makes it strikingly distinct, as the great majority of religions jostling for attention in our pluralistic age make not the slightest pretense of being objectively true in any verifiable manner. They are instead what Gene Veith accurately describes as "cultural religions," religions which serve primarily "to sanction social practices."[2] Many of Christianity's fundamental tenets, by contrast, are expressible in propositions capable of being verified or falsified by means of the rational weighing of evidence. To ask whether Jesus existed, or whether he publicly claimed to be God incarnate, or whether he rose from death to establish that claim is not at all to ask an esoteric "religious" question such as, "what is the sound of one hand clapping?" It is to ask a question about objective, historical facts.

It is therefore not surprising that the apostles themselves regularly appealed to empirical evidence in their proclamation of Christ.[3] John, for example, insists that he writes about what he and his companions "have heard, which we have seen with our eyes, which we looked upon and have touched with our hands" (1 John 1:1). Peter, in presenting the case for Christ to a skeptical, even hostile, audience, not only reminds his hearers that he was an eyewitness to the events described, but refers to these events having happened "as you yourselves know" (Acts 2:22). In similar fashion, the modern

---

[2] Gene Edward Veith, Jr., *The Spirituality of the Cross: The Way of the First Evangelicals* (St. Louis: Concordia, 1999), 92.

[3] See, e.g., F. F. Bruce, *The Defense of the Gospel in the New Testament* (Grand Rapids: Eerdmans, 1982).

apologist says merely, if there are certain objections to the faith which can be addressed by reasonable appeals to evidence—or certain foundational facts which can be similarly established—then, when speaking to the rational unbeliever, one should make every possible use of reason and evidence.

Nevertheless, many Christians, perhaps especially those Protestants within the Lutheran tradition (the tradition in which each of this volume's contributors stand), may remain wary of any confidence in or appeals to the utility of human reason. In our fallen state, it may be argued, the effects of sin inevitably prevent us from reasoning rightly in divine matters. Referencing Luther himself, one might further point out that this was the reformer's own conclusion, such that he could dismiss reason as "the greatest hindrance to faith,"[4] and "the devil's greatest whore."[5] The context of such pronouncements must ever be borne in mind, however, as it consistently reveals that Luther's objection is not to the use of reason *per se*, but to its use (or abuse) in speaking beyond or against divine revelation in theological matters. Thus, for example, when defending the clear proclamation of Scripture, he can be so bold as to say that "we must use our reason or else give way to the fanatics."[6]

Luther's positive regard for such a ministerial use of reason—subservient to, as well as in defense of, divine revelation—was not only clearly acknowledged, but also widely appropriated by the "orthodox fathers" of seventeenth-century Lutheranism, who thus allowed apologetic arguments to figure prominently in the

---

[4] Martin Luther, "Table Talk" (January 1533), in *D. Martin Luthers Werke: Kritische Gesamtausgabe, Tischreden*, 6 vols (Weimar: Hermann Böhlaus, 1912–21), 3:62 (no. 2904a).

[5] Martin Luther, "Sermon for the Second Sunday after Epiphany" (17 January 1546), in *D. Martin Luthers Werke: Kritische Gesamtausgabe*, 61 vols (Weimar: Hermann Böhlaus, 1883–1983), 51:126.

[6] Martin Luther, *Confession Concerning Christ's Supper* (1528), in *Luther's Works: American Edition*, 55 vols, ed. Jaroslav Pelikan and Helmut T. Lehmann (St. Louis: Concordia; Philadelphia: Fortress, 1955–86), 37:224.

prolegomena of their dogmatic works.[7] That the apologetic interest evident in early Lutheranism has waned in subsequent centuries— centuries in which the challenges to the Christian faith have greatly multiplied—has, we submit, benefited neither the Lutheran church nor the church universal, to say nothing of those yet outside the church. The contributors to the present volume, each of whom is a member of the Lutheran Church—Missouri Synod, evidence a continuing recognition of the utility of Christian apologetics as both an aid and complement to the church's evangelistic activities, perhaps not least because the cultural environment in which the church today finds itself differs so dramatically from that of Luther and his immediate theological heirs.

In view of this contemporary environment, the essays here gathered are intended to provide readers, particularly those who have had little introduction to or experience with apologetics, with a series of "case studies" in the discipline. As such, this work cannot pretend to be a comprehensive defense of the Christian faith; nor, conversely, is it meant to be a general introduction to apologetics, surveying various lines of defense in the absence of any particular context. Instead, in the fashion of case studies, the aim of each essay is to introduce readers to a specific intellectual objection to the Christian faith as exemplified by one or more influential contemporary thinkers, and then to demonstrate how this objection might rationally be answered and how counter-evidence and counter-argument might further substantiate the Christian assertion in question. Given the current popularity of many of the critics with whom this volume's contributors engage—often best-selling authors and speakers whose output is geared toward a non-professional audience; that is, the sorts of detractors whose arguments will very likely be familiar to the neighbor, co-worker, fellow-student, or even fellow-parishioner of most North American Christians—it is our hope that this collection of

---

[7] See, e.g., John Warwick Montgomery, "The Apologetic Thrust of Lutheran Theology," in *Theologia et Apologia: Essays in Reformation Theology and its Defense*, ed. Adam S. Francisco, Korey D. Maas, and Steven P. Mueller (Eugene, OR: Wipf & Stock, 2007), 5–21.

essays might in some modest manner better equip the faithful to defend their faith against any who would dismiss its proclamation as irrational or lacking evidence. Not that any might be "argued into faith"; but that by means of reasonable and persuasive argument, as by means of the law, "every mouth may be stopped" (Romans 3:19). And that, with mouths closed, way might be made for ears to be opened.

1

DEFENDING THE EXISTENCE OF GOD

Joshua Pagán

THE DEFENSE OF CHRISTIANITY

In the beginning, God created the heavens and the earth.

—Genesis 1:1

[T]he essential element in the astronomical and biblical accounts of Genesis is the same; the chain of events leading to man commenced suddenly and sharply, at a definite moment in time, in a flash of light and energy.

—Cosmologist Robert Jastrow[1]

Christianity is, philosophically speaking, monotheistic. Such a worldview essentially "says that the physical universe is not all there is. There is an infinite, personal God beyond the universe who created it, sustains it, and who acts within it in a supernatural way. He is transcendentally 'out there' and immanently 'in here.' "[2] Though monotheism has been intimately intertwined with the western worldview for more than two millennia, the western world has never been without those who would challenge the very existence of a personal God. In recent years, such challenges have emerged with notable conspicuity in the polemical writings of the "New Atheists." Arguably the most strident of such figures is evolutionary biologist Richard Dawkins, whose best-selling *The God Delusion* intends to demonstrate that the Christian belief system is, as its title indicates, "delusional." On Dawkins's assessment, religious commitment is more than a mere state of misguided belief; he does not mince words in his characterization of faith as a psychopathology:

---

[1] Robert Jastrow, *God and the Astronomers* (New York and London: W. W. Norton & Company, 1992), 14.

[2] Norman Geisler, *Baker Encyclopedia of Christian Apologetics* (Grand Rapids: Baker, 1999), 786.

The word "delusion" in my title has disquieted some psychiatrists who regard it as a technical term, not to be bandied about. Three of them wrote to me to propose a special technical term for religious delusion: "relusion". Maybe it'll catch on. But for now I am going to stick with "delusion", and I need to justify my use of it. The *Penguin English Dictionary* defines a delusion as "a false belief or impression.". . .

As to whether it is a symptom of a psychiatric disorder, I am inclined to follow Robert M. Pirsig, author of *Zen and the Art of Motorcycle Maintenance*, when he said, "When one person suffers from a delusion, it is called insanity. When many people suffer from a delusion it is called Religion."[3]

For Dawkins, and those within his camp of evangelistic atheism,[4] any theistic faith is an unfounded conviction that persists in the absence of sufficient evidence:

Faith is the great cop-out, the great excuse to evade the need to think and evaluate evidence. Faith is belief in spite of, even perhaps because of, the lack of evidence. . . . Faith is not allowed to justify itself by argument.[5]

But is this in fact the case? Can faith in the God of the monotheistic tradition be justified by empirical evidence or philosophical reasoning? The answer, quite certainly, is yes! This chapter shall be devoted to a discussion of the Kalam Cosmological Argument (KCA), an argument which lends substantial credence to

---

[3] Richard Dawkins, *The God Delusion* (London: Bantam Press, 2006), 5.

[4] Whereas "atheism" is typically understood as the categorical and absolute denial of God's existence, the term "nontheism" (which is gaining popularity within the secular community and in the sphere of philosophical-religious dialogue) shall be preferred throughout the body of this chapter.

[5] Dawkins is here quoted in a speech at the Edinburgh International Science Festival, April 15, 1992.

the "God-hypothesis" that Dawkins so vigorously attempts to refute. Regarded by many as the most cogent of the "classical" proofs for the existence of God, the Kalam Cosmological Argument successfully confers rational warrant upon theistic belief, despite typical atheistic critiques.

AN OVERVIEW
OF THE KALAM COSMOLOGICAL ARGUMENT

Named for the *kalam* tradition of Islamic discursive philosophy in which it was originally formulated,[6] the Kalam Cosmological Argument is a linear form of the cosmological argument that is frequently syllogized as follows:

1. All things that begin to exist have a cause.

2. The universe began to exist.

3. Therefore, the universe has a cause.[7]

---

[6] The Cosmological Argument is actually a category of arguments that seek to demonstrate the existence of a First Cause of the cosmos. In modern philosophical discourse, the Arabic word *kalam*, meaning "discussion" or "discourse," is used to designate the medieval Islamic version of the Cosmological Argument.

[7] Note the deductive form of this argument. If the major and minor premises are true, the terms are clear, and the rules of deductive reasoning are followed, then the conclusion is necessarily entailed. Quite remarkably, some critics of the KCA have claimed that the argument commits the fallacy of *petitio principii*, or "begging the question," by presupposing the truth of the conclusion in the first premise. This objection fails to understand that in a deductive argument, the conclusion is implicit in the premises and is derived by the rules of logical inference. In the foregoing formulation of the KCA, the rule of logical inference is a valid mechanism for the construction of a deductive proof known as *modus ponens*. (MP may be symbolically expressed as: If P then Q; P, therefore, Q.) Technically speaking, arguments do not actually "beg the question"; arguers do by affirming the truth of the first premise for the sole reason that the conclusion is *already* affirmed as true. The proponent

The KCA presents a truly formidable problem for those who would reject the God-hypothesis, perhaps especially in the twenty-first century. Prior to the late modern era, nontheists felt no compulsion to embrace the view that the cosmos came into existence *ex nihilo,* or "out of nothing," and therefore required a creator. When the timeless question of cosmic origins was posed, the nontheist could simply respond by proposing that the universe is *itself* eternal; it is a brute fact that always was and always will be.[8] Such an explanation regards the cosmos as a sort of factual necessity. In other words, it is not possible that our universe could ever have been nonexistent. This was the view of many ancient philosophers and was famously suggested also by the eighteenth-century skeptical empiricist David Hume, who asked, "why may not the material universe be the necessary existent Being?"[9]

The answer to Hume's query lies in the modern discovery that the universe almost certainly has *contingent,* rather than *necessary,* being.[10] The overwhelming evidence of twentieth-century

---

of the KCA affirms the truth of the first premise ("All things that begin to exist have a cause.") because it follows from the Principle of Sufficient Reason, not because of a prior affirmation of the conclusion ("Therefore, the universe has a cause.").

[8] The popular astrophysicist and cosmologist Carl Sagan, for example, began his highly-acclaimed PBS television series *Cosmos* stating, "The cosmos is all that is or ever was or ever will be." Bertrand Russell was persuaded of the same. In a BBC radio debate with Frederick Copleston, the late philosopher and mathematician stated, "The universe is just there, and that's all."

[9] David Hume, *Dialogues Concerning Natural Religion* (Charleston: Bibliobazaar, 2008), 72.

[10] As opposed to a necessary being, which can account for its existence by necessity of its own nature, a contingent being can only account for its existence by other than itself. This idea is expressed by a metaphysical law known as the Principle of Existential Causality, which states that every contingent being is caused, ultimately, by a necessary being. Further, while it is logically possible that a contingent being not exist, it is not logically possible that a necessary being not exist. Philosophers have found it useful to employ the concept of "possible worlds" to express

astrophysical investigation has given way to a revolutionary paradigm shift. Within the scientific community, therefore, it is now widely accepted that the cosmos *began* to exist, in the finite past, in an explosive event commonly termed the "Big-Bang."[11] Recent research has only confirmed this. In 2003, for example, physicists Arvin Borde, Alan Guth, and Alexander Vilenkin were able to prove that any universe which is (on average) expanding at a constant rate cannot be infinite in its past but must have a past space-time boundary.[12] On the implications of the Borde-Guth-Vilenkin singularity theorem (or BGV theorem), Vilenkin writes:

> It is said that an argument is what convinces reasonable men and a proof is what it takes to convince even an unreasonable man. With the proof now in place, cosmologists can no longer hide behind the possibility of a past-eternal universe. There is no escape, they have to face the problem of a cosmic beginning.[13]

When the results of modern scientific research are considered, those who would echo Hume's question are now forced to grapple with the idea that space, time, and cosmic matter came into existence as

---

modal claims concerning possibility, impossibility, and necessity. Here applied, it may be said that there exists a possible world in which any given contingent being does not exist, yet there exists no possible world in which a necessary being does not exist.

[11] As the famous theoretical physicist and cosmologist Stephen Hawking put it: "Almost everyone now believes that the universe, and time itself, had a beginning at the Big Bang." Stephen Hawking and Roger Penrose, *The Nature of Space and Time* (Princeton, NJ: Princeton University Press, 1996), 20.

[12] Arvin Borde, Alan Guth and Alexander Vilenkin, "Inflationary Space-Times are Not Past-Complete," *Physical Review Letters* 90 (2003), 1–4. It is significant to the present discussion that the BGV theorem holds regardless of the description of the early conditions of the universe, and applies equally to any tenable variant of multiverse theory.

[13] Alex Vilenkin, *Many Worlds in One* (New York: Hill and Wang, 2006), 176.

contingent realities that require a cause. If this ultimate cause is to explain the observed evidence and to avoid logical incoherencies, it must also be a metaphysically necessary, timeless, and personal cause.[14] In light of these attributes, the best explanation is that such a cause is an entity not at all unlike what theists refer to as God.

ALL THINGS THAT BEGIN TO EXIST HAVE A CAUSE: DEFENDING THE MAJOR PREMISE

The nontheist who denies the major premise of the KCA will find himself in an undoubtedly awkward position: if he accepts the Big-Bang theory (as Dawkins himself appears to),[15] he must also maintain that the universe came *from* nothing and was caused *by* nothing. Physicist Victor Stenger, for example, has proposed that the universe might have emerged from nothing as an uncaused entity.[16] But such a position is empirically deficient, if not completely nonsensical. Nowhere in human experience do events occur in the absence of an adequate cause, and it may therefore be understood that the major premise ("All things that begin to exist have a cause") is far more reasonable than its denial (*"Not* all things that begin to exist have a cause"). This follows from the philosophical Principle of Sufficient

---

[14] In the discourse of philosophy and theology, the term "personal" is normally understood to describe a being that is (at minimum) conscious and rational, possessing the faculties of intellect and will. Moreover, a being that is personal would also have *the potential* for interaction with other beings.

[15] In *The God Delusion*, 101, Dawkins proposes that a "big bang singularity" would be preferable to God as an explanatory cause of the universe. He writes, "To return to the infinite regress and the futility of invoking a God to terminate it, it is more parsimonious to conjure up, say, a 'big bang singularity', or some other physical concept as yet unknown."

[16] Victor Stenger, *Quantum Gods: Creation, Chaos, and the Search for Cosmic Consciousness* (New York: Prometheus Books, 2009), 73.

Reason.[17] When expressed in terms of causality, this principle states, "For every state of affairs *s*, if *s* obtains, then there is a sufficient reason or causal explanation for *s*." Even the aforementioned Hume admitted this, having remarked, "I have never asserted so absurd a proposition as that anything might arise without a cause."[18]

What is more, the entire scientific enterprise so vigorously defended by Dawkins fundamentally proceeds upon the closely related Principle of Causality; that is, "Nonbeing cannot cause being." The scientific axiom *ex nihilo nihil fit*, or "out of nothing, nothing comes" (i.e., nothing cannot bring about something), demands that nonbeing cannot give rise to that which has being. In the sheer absence of being there is no potency to generate any event or state of affairs. Without this First Principle of rational thought, descriptions of natural regularity, the construction of predictive models, and the acquisition of future knowledge would be impossible.[19] As noted above, modern cosmology has already proven beyond a reasonable doubt that the universe is an effect. By definition an effect is that which is caused; furthermore, an effect cannot be the cause of itself, as this would require that the effect be prior to itself.

Though the Principle of Causality appears self-evident, nontheists have attempted to deny it by various means. It has been suggested, for instance, that in the field of quantum physics certain subatomic events are known to occur as spontaneous and uncaused phenomena within the quantum vacuum. It is then surmised that the universe might have come into being in the same way. Yet this objection, scientists themselves understand, grossly miscomprehends the nature of the

---

[17] Be it within the field of science or the realm of philosophical discourse, an indubitable violation of the Principle of Sufficient Reason has yet to be furnished.

[18] *The Letters of David Hume, vol. 1, ed.* J. Y. T. Greid (Oxford: Oxford University Press, 1932), 187.

[19] Indeed, the entirety of human knowledge is ultimately grounded in the inviolable First Principles of rational thought. Apart from them, logical contradictions would preclude any possibility of true knowledge within the domain of science or any other field.

quantum vacuum and subatomic activity. The vacuum is not a complete void; rather, it is a quantum state of the lowest possible energy that yields spontaneous outcomes. "Even if the matter fields involved in the vacuum state are rather peculiar and certainly not observable in the sense that 'real' particles are, it is a mistake to think of any physical vacuum as some absolutely empty 'void'."[20] By no means, then, should the spontaneity of matter field activity be understood as the sudden or uncaused existence of matter *ex nihilo*.[21]

At times, Werner Heisenberg's Principle of Indeterminacy is also misinterpreted to undermine the Principle of Causality (and thereby, to reject the major premise of the KCA). Formulated from repeated experiments in quantum mechanics, Heisenberg's principle states that one cannot know the position *and* speed of a subatomic particle with complete certainty. "If one is known with a high degree of certainty, the other becomes very uncertain."[22] This idea of uncertainty is then applied to questions in metaphysics. It is posited that because events occur spontaneously and unpredictably at the subatomic level, not all events at the macro-level require causes.

Though psychologically convincing to some, such reasoning is again factually misinformed and logically fallacious. The Indeterminacy Principle essentially describes *the limitation of scientific observation capabilities* at the subatomic level; it should not be misconstrued as a demonstration that quantum events happen as uncaused phenomenon. The indeterminate nature of quantum activity is known to be a result of the observation process, rather than a property which is intrinsic to subatomic particles. Accordingly, Heisenberg's Principle of Uncertainty is to be properly understood as one of *unpredictability*, rather than one of *uncausality*. Even in the

---

[20] Christopher Ray, *Time, Space and Philosophy* (London and New York: Routledge, 1991), 205.

[21] See William Lane Craig, "Why I Believe God Exists," in *Why I Am a Christian: Leading Thinkers Explain Why They Believe*, ed. Norman L. Geisler and Paul K. Hoffman (Grand Rapids: Baker, 2001), 64.

[22] Alan Lightman and Roberta Brawer, *Origins: The Lives and Worlds of Modern Cosmologists*, (Cambridge: Harvard University Press, 1990), 560.

quantum world, the First Principles of logic dictate that one simply cannot get "something from nothing."

THE UNIVERSE BEGAN TO EXIST: DEFENDING THE MINOR PREMISE

The KCA proceeds with a contingent, value-neutral, existential fact: the universe began to exist. Nontheists who reject the Big-Bang model are forced to posit a variety of alternative cosmogonies.[23] Christian philosopher-theologian William Lane Craig observes, "Twentieth-century cosmology has witnessed a long series of failed attempts to craft plausible models of the expanding universe that avert the absolute beginning predicated by the standard model."[24] Such attempts have persisted into the twenty-first century. Though often inventive, competing explanations of cosmic origins want for evidential adequacy or logical coherence and, thus, are easily given to refutation.

For instance, intent on evading the need for an ultimate First Cause of the cosmos, advocates of the Eternal Universe hypothesis propose that because an infinite series of numbers is possible, so is an infinite series of past events or entities. Such analogical thinking is specious, however, as it neglects to consider a fundamental categorical distinction: whereas an infinite *mathematical* series is theoretical and abstract, an infinite *actual* series is real and concrete. As it concerns a series of actual entities or events, translation of the conceptually infinite to the empirically infinite results in intractable problems. As David Hilbert—who is widely regarded as the most influential mathematician of the twentieth century—bluntly asserted,

---

[23] For a sophisticated exposition of the KCA that includes a thorough and penetrating treatment of alternative cosmogonic models, see *The Blackwell Companion to Natural Theology*, eds. William L. Craig and J. P. Moreland (Chichester, UK: Wiley-Blackwell, 2012).

[24] William Lane Craig, "Theistic Critiques of Atheism," in *The Cambridge Companion to Atheism*, ed. Michael Martin (New York: Cambridge University Press, 2007), 78.

"The infinite is nowhere to be found in reality. It neither exists in nature nor provides a legitimate basis for rational thought. The role that remains for the infinite to play is solely that of an idea."[25] Simple thought experiments have repeatedly substantiated Hilbert's conclusion. For example, just because it is possible to posit an infinite number of abstract points between the covers of this book, this does not mean that an infinite number of pages (no matter how thin they may be) between the book's covers is actually possible. One could always add one more to an infinite actual series of entities or events, but this would make the series *more than* infinite in length, which is logically impossible.[26]

The Argument from Temporal Finitude further clarifies the absurdity of the Eternal Universe hypothesis. The argument may be expressed philosophically as follows:

1. If an infinite number of moments occurred prior to the present moment, then the present moment would never have arrived (because it is impossible to traverse an infinite number of moments).

2. But the present moment has come.

3. Thus, there were not an infinite number of moments before the present one, and the universe began a finite time ago.[27]

---

[25] David Hilbert, "On the Infinite," in *Philosophy of Mathematics*, ed. with and introduction by Paul Benaceraff and Hilary Putnam (Englewood Cliffs: Prentice-Hall, 1964), 139, 141.

[26] See further in Craig, "Theistic Critiques of Atheism," 77–78.

[27] Some have objected to the Argument from Temporal Finitude by attempting to point out that even in an infinite past, every past moment is only a finite distance from the present moment. Consider, as a thought experiment, that while the series of all negative numbers is without a beginning (. . . , -5, -4, -3, -2, -1, 0), any given number in the series is only a finite distance from zero. This objection commits the Fallacy of Composition, which arises when one mistakenly infers that a property is true of *the whole* from the fact that a property is true of *a part* of that

Further, *even if* an actual infinite series of past moments were possible, the finitude of the cosmos has, as previously noted, already been proven beyond a reasonable doubt.

Fundamentally similar to the Eternal Universe Hypothesis, yet even more untenable, is the Steady-State Hypothesis. Steady-State proponents also speculate that the universe has neither beginning nor end, but that, while constantly expanding, the universe maintains a constant average density (i.e., a steady-state) because matter continues spontaneously to come into existence. As this Steady-State model is both evidentially deficient and contrary to the Principle of Causality, it is no more viable than the preceding model. Indeed, it is far less viable. Again, no spontaneous materialization of matter has ever been observed in the universe, and so the intellectually honest scientist will refrain from submitting explanations which suffer from an utter absence of evidential corroboration, especially when the explanatory and predictive power of a competing hypothesis proves far superior. (In fact, due to its inferiority, the most prominent defense of the Steady-State, Fred Hoyle's, collapsed under the evidentiary weight of Big-Bang cosmology by the late1960s.) Moreover, the positing not only of a one-time spontaneous generation of something out of nothing, but of *continuous* generations *ex nihilo*, only multiplies the contradictions of the Principle of Causality.

Problematic for similar reasons is the Rebounding Universe Hypothesis, briefly considered and then dismissed by Einstein. Sometimes referred to as the Oscillating Universe Hypothesis, this model submits that what is typically referred to as *the* Big-Bang was only the most recent in an eternal series of expansions and collapses of the universe. Not only does this conjecture also fail for a lack of evidential support, but it further stands in contradiction of the Second

---

whole. Applied to the argument in question, we can say that just because every finite segment of an infinite number of moments can be traversed, it does not follow that the whole infinite number of moments can be traversed.

Law of Thermodynamics.[28] Implied by this inviolable principle of physics is that, even if the universe were constantly expanding and contracting in a series of "Big-Bangs" and "Big-Crunches," each successive rebound would grow longer with the effects of entropy. Working backward through previous oscillations, therefore, would entail their growing shorter and shorter—eventually culminating with a single, original Big-Bang. Thus, even if the universe were undergoing a perpetual process of expanding, contracting, and rebounding (which, again, is not borne out by any empirical evidence), it came originally into existence from nothing. Such *ex nihilo* emergence would still demand a metaphysically necessary First Cause.

Finally, many nontheists have attempted to avoid the need for an ultimate First Cause through some variant of Multiverse Theory, or Many Worlds Hypothesis (MWH). MWH imagines that our universe is but one of a randomly ordered and potentially infinite world ensemble that is generated by a mechanism of yet unknown scientific description.[29] While MWH has been given considerable attention in recent years, a number of significant deficiencies render it nonviable.

Because proponents of this model can furnish no empirical data in support of a world ensemble—or, for that matter, the presumably complex metalaws undergirding it—the MWH amounts to an exercise in philosophical speculation, rather than scientific explanation. With no observable evidence to be verified or falsified, MWH is at worst an *ad hoc*, quasi-scientific idea that is offered to rescue the possibility

---

[28] The Laws of Thermodynamics have significant implications for the ongoing discussion of cosmic origins. According to the Second Law, the amount of usable energy within a closed, isolated system (the amount of usable energy in the universe) is decreasing. Furthermore, when left to themselves, systems tend toward a state of maximum probability (which is chaos).

[29] Dawkins proposes that multiverse theory effectively answers the problem of "fine tuning" in the universe. For his brief discussion of MWH, see *The God Delusion*, 144–47.

of a strictly nontheistic account of the universe.[30] In fact, it may be argued that MWH actually suggests a distinctly theological category. Since an ensemble of worlds must exist beyond the boundaries of the scientifically detectible cosmos in which we find ourselves, it would be, by definition, *meta*physical—that is to say, beyond the physical nature of known reality. For this reason, the multiverse concept amounts to an impersonal, metaphysical hypothesis that is contrived to replace the personal, metaphysical hypothesis of God. Quite remarkably, advocates of MWH do not take issue with the idea of a metaphysical creator of the universe; it is the idea of a *personal, metaphysical* creator that cannot be permitted! Yet regardless of how one chooses to characterize the multiverse concept, because it has been shown that the past boundary point described by the BGV theorem applies equally to MWH, it fails to provide the past eternality hoped for by its supporters.[31] Simply put, all viable multiverse models still necessitate an ultimate beginning.

COSMIC ORIGIN AND DIVINE BEING:
DEFENDING THE NATURE OF GOD AS THE FIRST CAUSE

Some opponents of the God-hypothesis concede the finitude of the cosmos, as well as the metaphysical necessity of a timeless First Cause, yet attempt to maintain that this ultimate cause need not be a personal one. Such an objection, however, does not consider the logic of causality presupposed by the argument. If a timeless First Cause is to give rise to a temporal effect (such as the universe), it cannot simply be a non-volitional, mechanically operating set of necessary and sufficient conditions; if it were, the cause could never exist apart from its effect. Consider the following thought-experiment: at standard pressure, water begins to boil (the effect) because the temperature reaches one hundred degrees Celsius (the cause). But if the temperature were one hundred degrees Celsius from eternity past,

---

[30] Theism, in dramatic contrast, benefits from strong independent arguments and evidence that establish the feasibility of the God hypothesis.

[31] See above, n. 12.

then any water in existence would have been eternally boiling, and it would be impossible for the water to *have begun* to boil a finite time ago. So, if the cause is to be a timelessly present set of necessary and sufficient conditions, then the effect must be timelessly present also. In fact, there is only one way for a cause to be timeless while its effect is temporal; that is, the cause must be a personal agent who freely elects to create an effect in time without any prior determining conditions. For example, in contradistinction to the foregoing mental-exercise, an existentially free moral agent who had been standing from eternity past could freely decide, at some point in time, to sit down. In the final analysis, therefore, we are entirely warranted in concluding that the cause of the universe was a free creative act of an eternal personal being.

The personal nature of the First Cause may also be concluded by deductive reasoning alone. The Argument from First Cause may be stated as follows:

1. The cosmos is the effect of a First Cause.

2. The creative act of the First Cause was either determined, undetermined, or self-determined.

3. It cannot be determined, since there is nothing prior to the First Cause.

4. It cannot be undetermined, since this would contradict the Principle of Causality.

5. Hence, it must have been self-determined.

6. Yet self-determined acts are existentially free acts; that is to say, they are actions of existentially-free agents.

7. So, the creative act of the First Cause must have been the decision of an existentially-free agent.

At this point, the nontheist may be apt to object upon the basis of divine incoherence. "If the universe must have a First Cause," says the nontheist, "then so must God! What is the Cause of God?" Though such reasoning may appear sound *prima facie*, it betrays a lack of attention to the careful formulation of the KCA. The major premise of the argument does not propose, "All things that exist have a cause"; rather, it proposes, "All things that *begin* to exist have a cause." While the scientific evidence makes clear that the universe began to exist, classical theists have never suggested that God began to exist. In truth, a coherent doctrine of divine ontology demands that God must necessarily transcend space and time if he is to be the author of space and time. God's existence is not contingent upon anything apart from his own being; therefore, he does not require an existential cause. (He is Hume's "necessary being," which satisfactorily accounts for the recently discovered contingency of the universe.) On this point, it should not go unmentioned that the claim of eternality is not "special pleading" for God. Eternality is a quality which nontheistic thinkers had ascribed to the universe itself prior to the general acceptance of the Big-Bang model; if an ontologically necessary and timeless universe can be logically coherent, so also can an ontologically necessary and timeless personal being.

When speaking of God as the First Cause and best explanation of the universe, it must further be emphasized that the theist is not obligated to furnish an exhaustive explanation of God's ultimate origin. "The theist's answer," writes Dawkins, "is deeply unsatisfying, because it leaves the existence of God unexplained."[32] The presumption of such an obligation is also implicit in one of his central objections to the God-hypothesis. On his assessment, "the designer hypothesis immediately raises the larger problem of who designed the designer."[33] Theism, for Dawkins, fails to explain the advent and design of the universe for lack of a more foundational explanation of the designer.[34]

---

[32] Dawkins, *The God Delusion*, 143.

[33] Dawkins, *The God Delusion*, 158.

[34] In point of fact, it has already been established that a necessary being cannot have an origin. Further, if we can soundly infer the metaphysically necessary nature of God from the contingent nature of the universe, then arguments of probability and complexity have no force. A necessary being is by nature maximally probable. The critic would therefore be obliged to

Dawkins' "larger problem" betrays not only an egregious disregard of the theist's actual claim—that God, by definition, is a metaphysically necessary being, and as such has no designer—but even of the scientific framework in which any theory of origins must proceed. The scientific enterprise may be divided into two primary categories of investigation: *operation* and *origin* science. While operation science is an empirical discipline that deals with recurring patterns that are subject to experiment and observation, origin science is essentially a forensic discipline which investigates the past with special attention to singularities.[35] Since historical events cannot be tested and observed under the same controlled conditions as phenomena studied by operation science, historical circumstances, events, and entities must be reconstructed through the consideration of evidence and the techniques of historical method. Origin scientists accordingly employ a model of inductive reasoning known as "inference to the best explanation," or *abductive* reasoning. On the abductive model, historical descriptions are conceived upon the basis of accessible evidence and then tested in terms of explanatory power, explanatory scope, probability when compared to rival hypothesis, and other criteria. As a critical principle of origin science, an explanation need not have an explanation of itself to qualify as the best explanation of a past condition, event, or entity. (If such were the case, an infinite regress of explanations would result, and the explanatory process would never cease.) For this reason, the God-hypothesis does not fail for lack of a more foundational hypothesis; quite the contrary, it succeeds for having met the criteria of a sound historical explanation.

A brief scenario will help to illustrate this idea. Let us suppose that two archaeologists, Smith and Jones, are digging at an excavation site. Upon finding what clearly appears to be an ancient artifact, Smith would not tell his colleague, "By golly, Jones! Just look at the

---

prove the impossibility of a necessary being by demonstrating the incoherence of such a being.

[35] For further details, see Norman L. Geisler and J. Kirby Anderson, *Origin Science* (Grand Rapids: Baker, 1987).

way the sand has coalesced to form what appears to be a piece of pottery!" On the contrary, the archaeologists would theorize, with justification, that a (perhaps hitherto unknown) civilization left the artifact some time ago. The sufficiency of their explanation need not be dependent upon a more exhaustive knowledge of the economic conditions, religious life, or ultimate origin of the antiquated culture. Quite simply, *the archaeologist's conclusion is an inference to the best explanation of the evidence uncovered.* It is a simple, elegant hypothesis that is formulated upon analogical reasoning that artifacts are made by human beings.

One further comment on the nature and limitations of origin science is here warranted. Origin science is essentially a field of natural inquiry which seeks to describe past states of affairs in terms of antecedent and causal states of affairs. Because there quite simply was no natural state of affairs prior to the origins of the universe itself, the question of cosmic origins exceeds the actual scope of scientific investigation and must ultimately be deemed a *super*natural or metaphysical question. It was perhaps with this in mind that the great English scientist Sir Arthur Eddington remarked, "The beginning seems to present insuperable difficulties unless we agree to look on it as frankly supernatural."[36] If Eddington is correct, it would seem that an adequate account of the universe must permit consilience of science and theology as distinct yet complementary disciplines.

In a criticism that closely relates to the preceding, Dawkins contends that the assumed complexity of God counts against the probability of his existence and the explanatory power of the God-hypothesis. He intuits that a being capable of designing a universe such as our own "must be a supremely complex and improbable entity who needs an even bigger explanation than the one he is supposed to provide?"[37] To read this, one is inclined to believe that Dawkins defines complexity such that it could bear upon the ontological status

---

[36] Norman L. Geisler and Frank Turek, *I Don't Have Enough Faith to Be an Atheist* (Wheaton: Crossway, 2004), 85.

[37] Dawkins, *The God Delusion*, 147.

a metaphysical being. Analytic philosopher Alvin Plantinga finds this definition in *The Blind Watchmaker* (a work that Dawkins published in 1986) and responds as follows:

> So first, according to classical theology, God is simple, not complex. More remarkable, perhaps, is that according to Dawkins's own definition of complexity, God is not complex. According to his definition (set out in *The Blind Watchmaker*), something is complex if it has parts that are "arranged in a way that is unlikely to have arisen by chance alone." But of course God is a spirit, not a material object at all, and hence has no parts. *A fortiori* (as philosophers like to say) God doesn't have parts arranged in ways unlikely to have arisen by chance. Therefore, given the definition of complexity Dawkins himself proposes, God is not complex.[38]

Finally, a probative argument for the ontological simplicity of God may be advanced from his nature as the First Cause of the cosmos. Since God is the uncaused First Cause of the all things, it is logically impossible for there to have been any being prior to or beyond him to compose him. (And of course, a self-composed being would be logically incoherent.) As an uncomposed being, he cannot be decomposed. If he cannot be decomposed, then he must be simple. If he is simple, then he is not complex.[39]

---

[38] Alvin Plantinga, "The Dawkins Confusion: Naturalism ad absurdum," *Books & Culture: A Christian Review* (March/April 2007), 22.

[39] By Dawkins's own admission, a more simple theory is to be preferred over a more complex one. This principle, which is commonly referred to as "Occam's Razor," is expressed by the Latin phrase *pluralitas non est ponenda sine necessitate*, or "plurality should not be posited without necessity." As opposed to the naturalistic alternatives entertained by Dawkins, the God-hypothesis is a simple, elegant personal explanation of the finite nature (and observed complexity) in the universe.

DEFENDING THE EXISTENCE OF GOD

DEFENDING THEISM
BEYOND THE LIMITATIONS OF THE KCA

The soundness of the KCA and its conclusion thus appear evident; and yet, it is not uncommon for the argument to be judged unfavorably for its limitations. Theistic and nontheistic thinkers alike have alleged that although the argument may indeed prove the existence of God—an eternal, personal being—it says nothing, and can say nothing, of the divine attributes traditionally ascribed to him; to wit, omniscience, omnipotence, omnibenevolence, and such. In fact, Dawkins offers this criticism in his discussion of the Thomist Cosmological Argument:

> All three of these arguments rely upon the idea of a regress and invoke God to terminate it. They make the entirely unwarranted assumption that God himself is immune to the regress.[40] Even if we allow the dubious luxury of arbitrarily conjuring up a terminator to an infinite regress and giving it a name, simply because we need one, there is absolutely no reason to endow that terminator with any of the properties normally ascribed to God: omnipotence, omniscience, goodness, ...[41]

When responding to this objection, it is worth noting, first, that the KCA intends only to demonstrate the existence of a First Cause of the cosmos. Subsequent to this conclusion, one may then reason that a personal being whose properties are consistent with the God of Christian theism is the most coherent analysis and best explanation of that First Cause. (Much of this chapter has been devoted to this task.) Secondly, some traditional attributes *are in fact* implied by the nature of God as already established by the argument. Classical theism, for

---

[40] Dawkins completely ignores the fact that a metaphysically necessary being would certainly be immune from the problem of regress. Christian theism speaks of God's eternality in a *qualitative*, rather than *quantitative* sense. He is not an actual infinite series which would not be immune to the problem.

[41] Dawkins, *The God Delusion*, 77–78.

example, understands *aseity* (from Latin *a*, meaning "from," and *se*, meaning "self"), or "self-existence," to be among the essential divine attributes. Though Holy Scripture is often cited in support of this attribute, it may also be inferred wholly apart from special revelation.

Aseity is entailed by the nature of God as a necessary being. A necessary being cannot *not* exist and cannot exist in any way other than it necessarily does.[42] As such a being, God exists *a se*, or *in* and *of* himself. He does not *have* being; he *is* being, and thus contains within himself the explanation of his own existence. By necessity of his own nature, God is *pure actuality*; this is to say, absolutely no *potentiality* exists within his being. Whatever has potentiality must be effected or actualized by something other than itself. Since God is the ultimate and First Cause of the universe, there exists nothing prior to or beyond him to actualize any potential in his being. God cannot actualize his own potentiality to exist, for instance, as this would demand that he caused his own existence. It is metaphysically impossible for a being to be the cause of its own existence, as this would require that the being exist "prior to itself" (a logically incoherent notion).

Having established the attribute of aseity, we may now justifiably deduce that if God possesses any knowledge whatsoever, then he is perfectly knowledgeable (omniscient); if he possesses any power in

---

[42] It is not uncommon for opponents of theism to construe statements which delimit divine power as evidence against the God of Christian tradition. It is wrongly thought that since we may conceive a potential state of affairs that God cannot actualize (such as his own nonexistence), the concept of omnipotence is incoherent. But this essential attribute has been formulated such that the parameters of omnipotence are set without imposing any nonlogical constraint on God's power. Flint and Freddoso offer the following account of this essential attribute: "a person S is omnipotent at time t if S at t can actualize any state of affairs that is not described by counterfactuals about the free acts of others and that is broadly logically possible for someone to actualize, given the same hard past at t and the same true counterfactuals about the free acts of others." See T. Flint and A. Freddoso, "Maximal Power," in *The Existence and Nature of God*, ed. A. Freddoso (Notre Dame: University of Notre Dame Press, 1983), 81–113.

his being whatsoever, then he is perfectly powerful (omnipotent); and if he possesses any goodness in his being whatsoever, then he is perfectly good (omnibenevolent).[43]

CONCLUSION

In a 1992 publication titled *God and the Astronomers*, astrophysicist Robert Jastrow famously concluded, "For the scientist who has lived by his faith in the power of reason, the story ends like a bad dream. He has scaled the mountains of ignorance; he is about to conquer the highest peak; as he pulls himself over the final rock, he is greeted by a band of theologians who have been sitting there for centuries."[44] The picture painted by Jastrow is as intellectually honest as it is imaginative. Modern science has confirmed the position defended by biblical theologians throughout the history of Christianity: the universe is the creation of a metaphysically necessary, timeless, and personal First Cause. Rather than "belief in spite of, even perhaps because of, the lack of evidence," the most foundational commitment of the monotheistic worldview is strongly supported by the evidence of cosmological inquiry and the sound inferences of philosophical deduction. The opponents of theism have yet to submit an adequate defeater of the KCA, which testifies to its soundness as an empirically adequate and logical coherent defense of the Christian conviction that there does indeed stand behind the universe an eternal, personal, creative God.

---

[43] Upon considering this reasoning, a nontheist might remark, "Keep in mind that from this it follows from this that if God possesses any *evil* in his being, then he is perfectly evil!" This objection is defeated when a proper understanding of aseity is coupled with an Augustinian conception of evil as *privatio boni*, or "privation of the good." On Augustine's view, evil, unlike good, is insubstantial; that is, it is a deficiency (or absence) of the good, rather than entity or property that has ontic status. This metaphysical asymmetry considered, "evil" simply amounts to a name that we apply to privations of moral goodness. Since a being that exists *a se* (aseity) could in no way be deficient, it is impossible for God to be evil to any degree, let alone "perfectly evil."

[44] Jastrow, *God and the Astronomers*, 107.

FOR FURTHER READING

Berlinski, David. *The Devil's Delusion: Atheism and Its Scientific Pretensions*. New York: Crown Forum, 2008.

Coles, Peter. *Cosmology: A Very Short Introduction*. New York: Oxford University Press, 2001.

Craig, William L. *The Kalam Cosmological Argument*. London: MacMillan, 1979.

_____. *The Cosmological Argument from Plato to Leibniz*. London: MacMillan, 1980.

_____. *Reasonable Faith*. Wheaton: Crossway, 2008.

Flew, Antony, and Abraham Varghese. *There is a God: How the World's Most Notorious Atheist Changed His Mind*. New York: Harper One, 2007.

Geisler, Norman L. and Paul K. Hoffman, eds. *Why I Am a Christian: Leading Thinkers Explain Why They Believe*. Grand Rapids: Baker, 2001.

Lennox, John C. *God and Stephen Hawking*. Oxford: Lion Hudson, 2010.

_____. *God's Undertaker: Has Science Buried God?* Oxford: Lion UK, 2007.

McGrath, Alister. *The Dawkins Delusion: Atheist Fundamentalism and Denial of the Divine*. Downers Grove, IL: InterVarsity, 2007.

Copan, Paul and William Lane Craig. *Creation out of Nothing: A Biblical, Philosophical, and Scientific Exploration*. Grand Rapids: Baker, 2004.

Polkinghorne, John. *The Faith of a Physicist*. Minneapolis: Fortress Press, 1996.

2

The New Testament Gospels as Reliable History

Mark A. Pierson

INTRODUCTION

WHAT IS AT STAKE?

Did Jesus really do and say the things attributed to him in the New Testament? That is, are the canonical Gospels of Matthew, Mark, Luke, and John historically accurate reports of Jesus' words and deeds? Perhaps no single issue regarding the truthfulness of Christianity has received as much attention as this one. And it is easy to see why. Despite its profound and personally relevant doctrines, its uniquely coherent worldview, and its countless contributions to the betterment of mankind, Christianity ultimately amounts to a sham if the Jesus of history was (and is) not the same Jesus whose ministry, death, and resurrection are narrated in these texts. Simply put, if it can be shown that the New Testament is not historically reliable, Christianity will have been dealt a fatal blow.

Christianity is a historical religion, not just in the sense that it emerged, like other religions, at a particular point in history; rather, the central tenets of the Christian faith are inseparably linked to a historical person. The bedrock upon which all else rests is Jesus' action in history—primarily, what he taught about his own divine identity, and what he did to atone for sin. Everything that Christians believe is ultimately anchored to the person and work of a specific Jewish rabbi living under Roman rule in first-century Palestine. If, however, these biographical sketches of him are untrustworthy accounts, there remains little objective reason for believing that Jesus is the Christ, the Son of God, who has saved sinners by suffering as their substitute.[1] To remove the Gospels' chief stumbling block of

---

[1] Not surprisingly, Christians who ignore the issue of the Gospels' historicity typically rely on personal, subjective experiences as the basis for their faith, whereas those who keep the moniker "Christian" while reducing Jesus to something less than unique Lord and Savior invariably focus on his ethical teachings. In the former case, Christianity's truth claims can neither be verified nor falsified by objective facts, and are thus put on par with those of any other religion. In the latter case, alternate

"God crucified" is to reduce the Christian religion to just another ancient myth, or to regard it as a movement which scarcely represents the views of its obscure founder.

That Christians *do* believe in a mythical or legendary Jesus is precisely what skeptics have claimed for centuries, with ever-increasing intensity. Modern biblical scholarship, it is presumed, has exposed the glaring errors and irreconcilable problems in the New Testament texts, rendering them deficient sources for discovering the real Jesus.[2] The Gospels especially are routinely identified as biased products of the church rather than dependable reports of what truly happened. The current consensus in the academy as well as the media suggests that only those who shut their eyes and ears to the facts can maintain traditional beliefs about Jesus.

But have historians decisively determined that the Gospels are full of fiction? By no means. Scholars and apologists have perpetually demonstrated the texts' reliability by subjecting them to the same standards used for evaluating any work of ancient history. As a result, the form and content of the New Testament documents have often been praised for their remarkable accuracy.[3] Numerous skeptics, however, remain unconvinced by this approach and continue to denounce the veracity of the Gospels. Since their case often rests on the alleged findings of critical scholarship, it can appear credible and persuasive. Yet seldom is it recognized that their conclusions typically stem from unjustified starting points, and their assessment of the data is often unsound. We therefore first consider some of these questionable assumptions and methods before looking at the basics of the historical argument. In doing so, it will prove helpful to consider

---

versions of "Jesus" invariably have little to offer that cannot also be found in the teachings of Confucius, Muhammad, or certain talk show hosts.

[2] See *The Bible in Modern Culture: Baruch Spinoza to Brevard Childs*, 2d edition (Grand Rapids: Eerdmans, 2002).

[3] The classic volume on the subject remains F. F. Bruce, *The New Testament Documents: Are They Reliable?* (Grand Rapids: Eerdmans, 1960), though it should be supplemented with the more recent works suggested for further reading.

select arguments from one unbelieving scholar in particular: Bart Ehrman.

KNOW YOUR OPPONENT

Bart Ehrman fancies himself a jack-of-all-trades regarding biblical studies and speaks authoritatively on anything and everything relating to Jesus. He is also a former Christian who appears hell-bent on creating widespread doubt about the New Testament. Specifically, he popularizes various scholarly opinions that challenge what Christians believe. Though an erudite professor, he communicates in language that the average person can understand and regularly appeals to his own journey from faith to unbelief. This has made Ehrman immensely popular: some of his publications are used as college-level textbooks, while others have become *New York Times* best-sellers—a rare accomplishment for a New Testament specialist; he is also a media darling, with nearly every major outlet having featured (if not fawned over) his repudiation of Christianity.[4] For such reasons, Ehrman's skepticism warrants special attention as we assess the historicity of the Gospels.[5]

---

[4] Ehrman is also regularly cited by advocates of non-Christian views, including atheist Richard Dawkins (*The God Delusion* [New York: Houghton Mifflin, 2006], 95) and Muslim Louay Fatoohi (*The Mystery of the Historical Jesus: The Messiah in the Qur'an, the Bible, and Historical Sources* [Birmingham, UK: Luna Plena, 2007], 25–26).

[5] Critiques of Ehrman include Dillon Burroughs, *Misquotes in Misquoting Jesus: Why You Can Still Believe* (Ann Arbor: Nimble Books, 2006); Paul Timothy Jones, *Misquoting Truth: A Guide to the Fallacies in Bart Ehrman's Misquoting Jesus* (Downers Grove, IL: InterVarsity, 2007); and Daniel B. Wallace, "How Badly Did the Early Scribes Corrupt the New Testament? An Examination of Bart Ehrman's Claims" in *Contending with Christianity's Critics: Answering New Atheists and Other Objectors*, eds. Paul Copan and William Lane Craig (Nashville: B&H, 2009), 148–66.

PROLEGOMENA MATTERS

Where does one start in studying Jesus? Naturally, investigations are hindered when they are based on faulty premises, and conclusions are suspect if reliable procedures were not followed. For example, if one decides *a priori* that Jesus (or anyone else) never existed and then sets out to ascertain whether the documents which refer to him as a historical figure are credible, this will likely amount to proving what one's personal biases have already established. Evidence to the contrary will be distorted or ignored, as will the means by which such inquiries are routinely conducted. Thus, philosophical presuppositions regarding the nature of history and theology, speculations about the development of manuscripts, and the proper use of criteria all play a crucial role whenever someone examines the Gospels.[6] This is readily apparent in the views of Bart Ehrman.

MIRACLES, HISTORY, AND THEOLOGY

Ehrman is convinced that truly historical reports cannot include miraculous events. History only deals with "what *probably* happened. But by their very nature, miracles are highly *improbable* occurrences." When compared to all known historical claims, the sheer infrequency of miracle-claims is enough to render them "impossible."[7] In other words, only naturalistic explanations are plausible because they make up the bulk of human experience; miracles are precluded from historical reporting because of their anomalous and incredible character. By characterizing miracles and history in this mutually exclusive fashion, Ehrman has ruled out the

---

[6] On the relation of historiography and the Gospels, see N. T. Wright, *The New Testament and the People of God* (Minneapolis: Fortress, 1992), 81–144; William Lane Craig, *Reasonable Faith: Christian Truth and Apologetics*, 3d edition (Wheaton, IL: Crossway, 2008), 207–45; and Michael R. Licona, *The Resurrection of Jesus: A New Historiographical Approach* (Downers Grove, IL: InterVarsity, 2010), 29–132.

[7] Bart D. Ehrman, *Jesus: Apocalyptic Prophet of the New Millennium* (Oxford: Oxford University Press, 2001), 227–28; italics original. By permission of Oxford University Press, Inc.

supernatural from the start. "Even if there are otherwise good sources for a miraculous event, the very nature of the historical discipline prevents the historian from arguing for its probability."[8] It is no wonder, then, that he discounts all reports of miracles when gauging what can be known about Jesus; they are simply deemed *ahistorical*.

With this line of reasoning, Ehrman essentially echoes David Hume, who argued that observations of the past consist almost entirely of ordinary, mundane happenings, while miraculous "facts" are exceedingly rare by comparison.[9] Moreover, since experience teaches that people deceive and are misled on a regular basis, it is always more prudent to distrust witnesses who support miracle-claims than it is to believe the miracles happened.[10] Thus, Hume claimed that even if a naturalistic explanation is weak and preposterous, it nevertheless remains more plausible than a supernatural one.

However, one must be careful not to let bad philosophy corrupt good history. Why should a miracle-claim be considered improbable if it is the best explanation of all available evidence? If the alleged miracle occurred within a significant religious context, if the data supporting it is strong, and if alternative explanations are weak and unreasonable, then the likelihood of a genuine miracle should not be patently rejected. Hume and Ehrman would have us believe that an investigation of the facts is simply unnecessary because miracles, by definition, are too far-fetched to be treated as "regular" history. But this can only be known if the historical reliability of all miracles has already been examined and found to be inadequate or defective.[11] Historians ought to build their case inductively by letting the facts

---

[8] Ehrman, *Jesus*, 196. "I wish we could establish miracles, but we can't. It's no one's fault. It's simply that the cannons [sic] of historical research do not allow for the possibility of establishing as probable the least probable of all occurrences." By permission of Oxford University Press, Inc. Quoted in Licona, *The Resurrection of Jesus*, 174.

[9] David Hume, *An Inquiry Concerning Human Understanding*, ed. Charles W. Hendel, reprint (New York: The Liberal Arts Press, 1957), 124–25.

[10] Hume, *An Inquiry Concerning Human Understanding*, 126, 138.

[11] See Licona, *The Resurrection of Jesus*, 135–53.

speak for themselves, not start from a particular worldview that makes it impossible to know if supernatural events have ever occurred.[12]

Another of Ehrman's assumptions is that because the Gospel writers were motivated by theological concerns, they could not have produced reliable history. It is true that Matthew, Mark, Luke, and John were not interested in recording names and events merely for the sake of posterity. As followers of Jesus, their narratives were composed with the intent of teaching the religious significance of what had occurred. According to Ehrman, this disqualifies them from being trustworthy sources; historians "cannot presuppose belief or disbelief in God" without necessarily compromising their objective approach to the data.[13] The moment any would-be chronicler of events reveals his own religious biases, he effectively ceases to practice the historian's craft and has entered the realm of theology or philosophy.

This is a fairly stunning contention coming from Ehrman, who claims to be a historian himself yet customarily begins his popular books with a personal account of how he came to lose faith in Jesus and reject the divine origin of Scripture.[14] His works are often saturated with his personal vendetta against Christianity. By his own rationale, this theological (or, *anti*-theological) agenda taints his

---

[12] Scathing critiques of Hume on miracles include *In Defense of Miracles*, eds. R. Douglas Geivett and Gary Habermas (Downers Grove, IL: InterVarsity, 1997), and John Earman, *Hume's Abject Failure: The Argument against Miracles* (Oxford: Oxford University Press, 2000).

[13] Quoted in Licona, *The Resurrection of Jesus*, 173.

[14] Bart D. Ehrman, *Misquoting Jesus: The Story Behind Who Changed the Bible and Why* (New York: HarperCollins, 2005), 1–15; idem, *God's Problem: How the Bible Fails to Answer Our Most Important Question—Why We Suffer* (New York: HarperCollins, 2008), 1–19; idem, *Jesus, Interrupted: Revealing the Hidden Contradictions in the Bible (and Why We Don't Know about Them)* (New York: HarperCollins, 2009), ix–18, 273–78; idem, *Forged: Writing in the Name of God—Why the Bible's Authors Are Not Who We Think They Are* (New York: HarperCollins, 2011), 1–11, 115–17.

approach to the New Testament, placing him in the same camp as the Gospel authors whom he accuses of being pseudo-historians.[15]

The notion that a historian can completely purge himself of private opinions or vested interest regarding his subject is simply naïve. These will always influence how the data is interpreted and how much weight is given to specific points—especially when matters of religion are involved. However, if the reporter witnessed the events firsthand, consulted others who did, or used reliable sources, his account remains valuable regardless of whether his personal beliefs were incorporated. Richard Whately's satirical *Historic Doubts Relative to Napoleon Bonaparte* demonstrates the futility of abandoning all testimony that contains bias.[16] Whately, attempting to write a strictly factual biography of the French leader, accepted only impartial viewpoints as dependable. Since no material met this stringent requirement, Whately, whose work was published while Napoleon was still alive, was forced to conclude that Napoleon never existed! Consider similarly the few people inside the World Trade Center who survived the terrorist attacks of September 11. Their unique experiences should not simply be dismissed if they happen to contain expressions of proud patriotism or heartfelt grief, or even if they attribute their survival to divine providence.

There is no justifiable reason to separate history and theology into watertight compartments such that overlap between the two is impossible. Richard Bauckham has convincingly shown that eyewitness testimony is precisely "where history and theology

---

[15] Apparently, Ehrman thinks he is immune from his own judgment: "It is sometimes possible to detect a clear bias in an author—for example, when just about every story in his or her account drives home, either subtly or obviously, the same point. . . . Whenever you can isolate an author's biases, you can take them into account when considering his report. That is to say, statements supporting his bias should then be taken with a pound of salt (not necessarily discarded, but scrutinized carefully)." Ehrman, *Jesus*, 89. By permission of Oxford University Press, Inc.

[16] This work is reprinted in Craig Parton, *Richard Whately: A Man For All Seasons* (Edmonton, Alberta: Canadian Institute for Law, Theology, and Public Policy, 1997).

meet."[17] In fact, "all history, like all knowledge, relies on testimony," and should be trusted or distrusted based on the evidence.[18] Since the Gospels claim to record God's actions in human history through the person of Jesus, their theological connotations should not prevent them from being judged on their historical merits. Indeed, this may even enhance their trustworthiness. As New Testament scholar Mark Roberts declares: "I am motivated all the time by a theological passion that calls me to be a faithful historian."[19] Thus, Ehrman's staunch skepticism is not only unfounded; it actually hinders one from acquiring knowledge of the past.

ABUSES OF FORM AND REDACTION CRITICISMS

Two of the most commonly used methods for studying the Gospels have been form criticism and redaction criticism.[20] Like any tools, they can yield some helpful results when properly applied; but they can also be abused. Form criticism tries to discern the oral traditions employed by each author, given that the good news was proclaimed before any of the Gospels were composed. This can help determine a text's different "forms," allowing each distinct section to be interpreted according to its genre, and shedding light on the narrative's overall structure. Parables, for example, are not to be taken as literal history, and the arrangement of Jesus' parables often accentuates their meanings. The danger arises when it is presumed

---

[17] Richard Bauckham, *Jesus and the Eyewitnesses: The Gospels as Eyewitness Testimony* (Grand Rapids: Eerdmans, 2006), 6. See also I. Howard Marshall, *Luke: Historian and Theologian*, 3d edition (Downers Grove, IL: InterVarsity, 1988), 13–52.

[18] Bauckham, *Jesus and the Eyewitnesses*, 5.

[19] Mark D. Roberts, *Can We Trust the Gospels? Investigating the Reliability of Matthew, Mark, Luke, and John* (Wheaton, IL: Crossway, 2007), 121.

[20] See Craig Blomberg, *The Historical Reliability of the Gospels*, 2d edition (Downers Grove, IL: InterVarsity, 2007), 48–75. For primers on these disciplines, see E. V. McKnight, *What is Form Criticism?* (Philadelphia: Fortress, 1969), and Dan O. Via, *What is Redaction Criticism?* (Philadelphia: Fortress, 1969).

that the oral traditions were substantially altered before being transcribed. In particular, it is regularly supposed that a Gospel contains not so much the truth about Jesus but the beliefs of the anonymous community in which it developed. Some scholars have therefore compared the Gospels with folklore—material developing over numerous generations and throughout large geographic areas, without definite concerns for historical accuracy.

Ehrman employs this model, stating that a "community's traditions reflect the events that have happened in the meantime"; that is, between the time of Jesus and the completion of a Gospel, the stories were altered to fit the community's needs. This approach makes it possible to explain "why they told the stories about Jesus as they did."[21] Take Jesus' divinity in John's Gospel, for instance. Ehrman says John's community "started thinking of Jesus in more exalted terms to explain their own rejection by the synagogue." So by the time the fourth Gospel was written,

> the author incorporated a range of traditions that had been circulating among them, both those that were their original views, in which Jesus was fully human, and those that came later, in which he was himself divine. And thus there developed the view that Jesus was God.[22]

Jesus' claims to deity are therefore systematically written off as having been placed into his mouth years later by the community.

The community model, however, is merely assumed, and rests on no substantial argument.[23] Evidence suggests that early Christian leaders traveled to various churches; and the Gospel authors need not have lived in only one community while composing their texts. Constant, close communication existed between Christians, keeping

---

[21] Ehrman, *Jesus, Interrupted*, 250.

[22] Ehrman, *Jesus, Interrupted*, 252.

[23] Richard Bauckham, "For Whom Were Gospels Written?" in *The Gospels for All Christians: Rethinking the Gospel Audiences*, ed. Richard Bauckham (Grand Rapids: Eerdmans, 1998), 11.

them from isolation and preventing them from injecting novel ideas into their beliefs.[24] If the Gospels were written for general circulation, as is most likely, then attempting to identify which parts of the text resulted from local concerns is misguided. Even if the Gospels were written for particular churches, sifting out the genuine pieces of tradition from what was supposedly added by anonymous communities will necessarily rely on conjecture. Worse still, "There is a circularity inherent in interpreting the texts in the light of hypothetical communities, the nature of which has already been deduced solely from the texts!"[25]

Ehrman also likens the Gospels to American folklore—specifically, to the tale of George Washington cutting down a cherry tree. This story was made up as "national propaganda," and is told "to convey an important lesson in personal morality." The Gospels, he asserts, served a similar function; they "contain stories that may convey truths, at least in the minds of those who told them, but that are not historically accurate."[26]

Here we see a customary mixing of apples and oranges, the employment of a false analogy. The Gospels simply do not resemble folklore, American or otherwise. Classicist Richard Burridge has compared them with a diverse collection of Greco-Roman biographies, noting unmistakable similarities in both structure and substance, and concluding that the proper genre of the Gospels is ancient biography.[27] This means they purport to contain truthful information about a person, not merely abstract ideas or theological instructions based on legends. Since knowing a text's genre is crucial for interpretation, Ehrman's reading of the Gospels is fundamentally flawed.

---

[24] See Bauckham, "For Whom Were Gospels Written?," 30–44.

[25] Richard A. Burridge, "About People, By People, For People: Gospel Genre and Audiences," in *The Gospels for All Christians*, 126.

[26] Ehrman, *Jesus*, 30, 31. By permission of Oxford University Press, Inc.

[27] See Richard A. Burridge, *What Are the Gospels? A Comparison with Greco-Roman Biography*, 2d edition (Grand Rapids: Eerdmans, 2004).

Redaction criticism deals with each text as a completed whole, as opposed to its hypothetical development. Specifically, each author is regarded as a deliberate editor (or, redactor) who selected, arranged, and rephrased his material based on his distinct theological perspective. Despite variations, which have been well-known since at least the second century, Christians have always preferred four separate Gospels rather than one fully harmonized memoir.[28] Having multiple witnesses not only enhances our understanding of Jesus, but also provides greater credibility for the events they record.[29] Redaction criticism has increased respect for the authors as talented composers of cohesive narratives, each stressing particular aspects of Jesus' significance; but problems emerge when the Gospels' similarities are downplayed and their differences are exaggerated. For Ehrman, certain of these differences show "historical inaccuracies" which "simply cannot be reconciled without doing violence to the text."[30] He offers a handful of examples to demonstrate how the writers often "made a slight change in a historical datum to score a theological point."[31] In other words, if it furthered their theological agenda, they willingly fudged the facts.

Space precludes looking at each supposed contradiction in detail, but plausible solutions for two of them will be noted here.[32] First, the utterance from heaven at Jesus' baptism is not exactly the same in Matthew, Mark, and Luke. According to Ehrman, the writers changed or invented the episode for divergent theological reasons, forever

---

[28] Toward the end of the second century, Tatian produced such a harmony called the *Diatessaron*; it remained in use a relatively short time.

[29] A list consisting of thirty-three basic details "about Jesus' life and ministry that are found in *all four Gospels*—yes, including John" is provided in Roberts, *Can We Trust the Gospels?*, 97–100; emphasis original.

[30] Ehrman, *Jesus*, 35. By permission of Oxford University Press, Inc.; idem, *Jesus, Interrupted*, 22.

[31] Ehrman, *Jesus*, 35. By permission of Oxford University Press, Inc.

[32] On supposed contradictions, see Gleason L. Archer, *New International Encyclopedia of Bible Difficulties* (Grand Rapids: Zondervan, 1982).

obscuring what really occurred.[33] But in the ancient world, historians were more concerned with preserving someone's actual voice (*ipsissima vox*) than their actual words (*ipsissima verba*); paraphrase was sufficient as long as it faithfully captured the sense of what was said. (The import of this practice becomes especially apparent when we consider that Jesus likely spoke in Aramaic—at least much of the time—while all four Gospels were written in Greek.) Thus, different renditions of someone's original speech need not match word-for-word to be considered reliable.[34]

Second, Ehrman's favorite example of a theologically motivated error is the date and time of the crucifixion given by John.[35] Mark 15:25 clearly states that Jesus was nailed to the cross on the day of Passover (Friday). Yet John 19:14 says that Jesus was crucified the day *before* Passover (Thursday). Ehrman explains this discrepancy by focusing on a designation for Jesus that is unique to the fourth Gospel: the Lamb of God (1:29, 36). John, Ehrman argues, wanted to portray Jesus as the Passover lamb of Exodus, whose shed blood turned away God's wrath. In the first century, when Jews reenacted this sacred meal each year, the lambs were slaughtered *before* Passover, on the day of Preparation. Obviously, the actual date of Jesus' death was changed by John to stress its theological significance.[36] Or, was it?

New Testament professor Craig Blomberg has examined the various attempts to reconcile Mark and John on this point, and suggests a fairly straightforward solution. John 19:14 begins, "Now it

---

[33] Ehrman, *Jesus, Interrupted*, 39–40, 52–53.

[34] See Darrell L. Bock, "The Words of Jesus in the Gospels: Live, Jive, or Memorex" in *Jesus Under Fire: Modern Scholarship Reinvents the Historical Jesus*, eds. Michael J. Wilkens and J. P. Moreland (Grand Rapids: Zondervan, 1995), 73–99.

[35] Ehrman refers to it habitually, and it is the foremost example in his college-level textbook, *The New Testament: A Historical Introduction to the Early Christian Writings*, 4th edition (New York: Oxford University Press, 2008), 262–65.

[36] Ehrman, *Jesus, Interrupted*, 23–27.

was the day of Preparation of the Passover," which is assumed to mean the day before Passover itself. But in context, Blomberg notes, " 'the Passover' could just as easily mean the week-long festival," not just the one day itself. He likewise observes that " 'the day of Preparation' could mean Friday (the day of preparation for the Sabbath),"[37] because both 'preparation' and 'Friday' are expressed by the same Greek word (*paraskeuē*). In every other place in the New Testament where this word is used, including twice in John, it clearly means the day before the Sabbath. Thus, "it is completely appropriate to understand John to mean that 'it was Friday of Passover week.' "[38] What appeared at first glance as a theologically-driven manipulation of the facts is explained quite reasonably.

MISHANDLING THE CRITERIA OF AUTHENTICITY

One of the standard positions held in the academy is that the New Testament authors transformed the Jesus of history (the real Jesus) into the exalted Christ of faith (the Jesus worshipped by later Christians). It is simply not accepted that they are one and the same person. Therefore, various "quests" for the so-called "historical Jesus" have tried to strip away the layers of dogma found in the Gospels and reconstruct the long-concealed man from Nazareth.[39] As Ehrman explains, the goal is to "get behind the theologically molded accounts to uncover the actual events that lie underneath them."[40] Building upon this premise, Ehrman also claims that accounts "clearly imbued with a highly developed theology are less likely to be historically accurate."[41] He reasons these could only have been

---

[37] Craig Blomberg, *The Historical Reliability of John's Gospel: Issues and Commentary* (Downers Grove, IL: InterVarsity, 2001), 246–47.

[38] Craig Blomberg, *The Historical Reliability of John's Gospel*, 247.

[39] For an excellent summary of these quests, see the introduction of *The Historical Jesus: Five Views*, eds. James K. Beilby and Paul Rhodes Eddy (Downers Grove, IL: InterVarsity, 2009), 9–54.

[40] Ehrman, *Jesus*, 36. By permission of Oxford University Press, Inc.

[41] Ehrman, *Jesus*, 88. By permission of Oxford University Press, Inc.

formulated after much reflection, which makes them late and unreliable.

Inherent in this approach is the assumption that much of what Jesus actually said and did either was forgotten or was unimportant compared to what was invented about him afterward. But if Jesus made virtually no impact on his followers, it is remarkable that the Gospels should exist at all. Craig Evans, an expert on historical Jesus studies, considers it "absurd" to suggest that Jesus was unmemorable or kept incompetent disciples.[42] "Had there been no messianic content in Jesus' teaching and activities prior to Easter, it is doubtful that there would have been any after Easter."[43] In light of this point, we must wonder why Jesus' original words could not have included what Ehrman considers "highly developed theology." If Jesus actually claimed to be one with God (John 10:30), instructed his disciples to baptize in the name of the Father, Son, and Holy Spirit (Matthew 28:19), and explained that he would give his life as a ransom for many (Mark 10:45), then the earliest theology *is* the highest theology—there was no need for it to develop. That is not to say everyone immediately grasped the significance of Jesus' identity and mission; but it is imprudent to judge elements of the Gospels as early or late, and therefore as historical or fabricated, based on their theological import.

Despite many scholars trying to discover a Jesus different than the one presented in the Gospels, some criteria employed to determine the authenticity of his sayings and actions can be helpful—to an extent.[44] The most famous of these is the criterion of "double dissimilarity," which tries to isolate anything in the Gospels which

---

[42] Craig A. Evans, *Fabricating Jesus: How Modern Scholars Distort the Gospels* (Downers Grove, IL: InterVarsity, 2006), 47. See also James D. G. Dunn, *A New Perspective on Jesus: What the Quest for the Historical Jesus Missed* (Grand Rapids: Baker, 2005), 28–34.

[43] Evans, *Fabricating Jesus*, 46.

[44] Certain positive and negative criteria are explained in Robert H. Stein, "Criteria for the Gospels' Authenticity," in *Contending with Christianity's Critics*, 88–103.

deviates from the Judaism of Jesus' day *and* from primitive Christianity. If material is distinct from both traditions, this leaves Jesus himself as the most likely source. Though there is a definite logic to this criterion, it has very limited value: the Jesus it uncovers is necessarily unjewish and unchristian. Since Jesus was a devout Jew whose followers made up the Early Christian Church, this is clearly problematic.

Ehrman's understanding of such criteria not only appears misguided, but his application of their findings is often arbitrary, if not disingenuous. In three examples of how "double dissimilarity" is applied, he actually uses an altogether different criterion instead—that of "embarrassment." The "embarrassment" criterion identifies awkward material that could have hindered the Christian message, but was retained because it actually happened. The examples Ehrman cites are Jesus' baptism by John (which could imply that Jesus was John's subordinate), Jesus' betrayal by a close friend (which might have made Jesus look gullible or weak), and Jesus' death by crucifixion (a most scandalous fate for the Messiah).[45] While all of these do meet the criterion of "embarrassment" none satisfies the criterion of "double dissimilarity," casting doubt on Ehrman's command of the issues.

More significantly, Ehrman inverts these positive criteria such that they become restrictive principles. He is unwilling to affirm much of anything in the Gospels as genuine unless multiple criteria are satisfied, yet the benchmark of which ones or how many is never specified. For example, Jesus' birth in Bethlehem of a virgin mother meets the criterion of "multiple attestation," for Matthew and Luke both relied on separate, independent sources for their material (that is, neither author borrowed from the other). The accounts, however, are not dissimilar to early Christian beliefs, so Ehrman concludes: "Some of the best known traditions of Jesus' birth cannot be accepted as historically reliable when gauged by our criteria."[46] Or again, while

---

[45] Ehrman, *Jesus*, 93.

[46] Quoted in Craig, *Reasonable Faith*, 293.

Jesus' baptism by John meets the criterion of "embarrassment," John's reluctance is discounted because it is not multiply attested, making it "appear to be suspect."[47] For Ehrman, failing to meet one of the criteria, even while meeting others, has become evidence for inauthenticity. This, however, is not how the positive criteria work: satisfying even one of them only *increases* the probability that the passage is authentic.[48] If Ehrman's method was implemented by scholars when studying other ancient historical writings, the vast majority of accepted history would have to be jettisoned.

Having noted how bad approaches to the texts can affect one's conclusions, we now turn to the standard historical argument. For this, it should be remembered that we are merely treating the Gospels like any documents from antiquity: no special pleading; no double-standards; and no predetermined outcome.

THE HISTORICAL ARGUMENT

To determine what happened in the past, thoughtful scholars ask questions that aid in assessing the historical value of ancient documents, such as: Who wrote this, and when? Would the author have had access to reliable data? Do external sources confirm authorial claims? Has the text been accurately preserved? For the Gospels, each individual question could (and does) generate entire books. We merely consider the questions according to three categories: the integrity of texts themselves; the reliability of their content; and extra-biblical support.

THE MANUSCRIPT EVIDENCE

Prior to the invention of the printing press, every copy of every New Testament book was handwritten. While most copyists were professional scribes, they were also fallible humans who could have altered the text—either accidentally or intentionally. Since the

---

[47] Ehrman, *Jesus*, 93. By permission of Oxford University Press, Inc.

[48] Stein, "Criteria for the Gospels' Authenticity," 102.

meticulous but imperfect practice of copying went on for centuries, it is reasonable to wonder whether the Gospels we have today resemble what was originally written. The discipline of evaluating these copies is called textual criticism. A textual critic essentially compares reproductions of the same manuscript, notes the variants between them, and attempts to reconstruct the original based on this information. The process is so straightforward that it has been called the "most objective" aspect of New Testament studies.[49] This also happens to be Bart Ehrman's area of expertise, from which he condemns the Gospels as having been corrupted during the transmission process. He claims the copies have more variants than actual words; he says scribes changed wording to promote particular theologies; and he offers examples where the original reading of the text remains uncertain.[50] Those unfamiliar with textual criticism are often surprised and troubled by these statements, which is precisely what Ehrman intends. However, all the available data actually *increases* confidence in the Gospels.

Textual critics judge the integrity of manuscripts, in part, according to the following criteria: how old the copies are in relation to the original; how many copies are available for comparison; and how significant the variants are.[51] As far as we know, the original Gospel manuscripts ("autographs") have been lost to the sands of time. What textual critics want, then, are copies that date as near to the autographs as possible, which reduces the number of alterations that could have been introduced. We will say more about the dating of the Gospels below, but for now it suffices to note that virtually all scholars think they were composed during the second half of the first century.

---

[49] Roberts, *Can We Trust the Gospels?*, 32–33.

[50] Ehrman, *Misquoting Jesus*, 90, 133–48, 155–75.

[51] For other standards and methods, see Kurt Aland and Barbara Aland, *The Text of the New Testament: An Introduction to the Critical Editions and to the Theory and Practice of Modern Textual Criticism*, 2d edition, trans. Erroll F. Rhodes (Grand Rapids: Eerdmans, 1989), 280–316.

The earliest existing Gospel manuscripts are individual papyrus fragments that have been dated as early as AD 125—only a couple of generations after the originals.[52] Though that may seem like a long time, two points should be kept in mind. First, the autographs themselves, as well as any immediate copies, could have lasted a hundred years or more before the papyrus wore out. If these were still being circulated, read, and copied during that time, they would have served to safeguard against significant modifications. This means our earliest manuscripts would have been produced when the autographs were still in use, effectively making the time gap immaterial.[53] Second, the time between our first copies of the Gospels and the autographs is minimal compared to other works of antiquity. Five hundred years separate the classic Greek historians Herodotus and Thucydides from the oldest known copies of their works. The earliest texts from Roman historians Tacitus and Suetonius, both of whom wrote shortly after the Gospels, come from the ninth century. Similarly, the Jewish historian Josephus wrote in the first century, but no copy of his work dates before the eleventh century—a thousand years later! Nevertheless, classicists and historians still consider these reliable sources for learning about the past.[54]

The number of copies of the Gospels is likewise impressive when compared to other ancient writings. If we consider only those in Greek (though many more are in Latin and other languages), we have about twenty times more Gospel manuscripts than the average number for any work from the Greco-Roman world.[55] To place the

---

[52] See Evans, *Fabricating Jesus*, 26, 32–33.

[53] Craig A. Evans, "Can We Trust the Bible on the Historical Jesus?" (paper presented at the annual Greer-Heard conference, New Orleans Baptist Theological Seminary, February 25–26, 2011), forthcoming as "Can We Trust what the New Testament Says about the Historical Jesus?" in a book edited by Robert B. Stewart.

[54] See J. Ed Komoszewski, M. James Sawyer, and Daniel B. Wallace, *Reinventing Jesus: How Contemporary Skeptics Miss the Real Jesus and Mislead Popular Culture* (Grand Rapids: Kregel, 2006), 71.

[55] Roberts, *Can We Trust the Gospels?*, 31.

same individuals mentioned above in descending order, there are two hundred copies of Suetonius, one hundred thirty-three of Josephus, seventy-five of Herodotus, twenty of Thucydides, and three of Tacitus.[56] For the Gospels, however, there are over two thousand total manuscripts. In fact, the earliest Christians cited the Gospels so frequently in sermons, lectionaries, letters, and apologetic works, that even if every early edition of the Gospels was destroyed, we could effectively reconstruct them in their entirety.[57] All this puts us in a tremendous position for determining the original wording. Most interestingly, Ehrman has admitted as much. In a book co-authored with Bruce Metzger, the foremost textual critic of the twentieth century, they concluded that "the textual critic of the New Testament is embarrassed by the wealth of material."[58]

Concerning the variants themselves, the situation is nowhere near as dire as Ehrman makes it seem. Yes, there are thousands of variants, even more variants than words, but this is due to the excessive number of manuscripts. (One naturally expects to find more variants in the thousands of copies of the Gospels than in the three of Tacitus.) For example, the Gospel of Mark consists of 11,260 Greek words. If a scribe introduced 25 variants into his copy of Mark, he would have averaged one mistake every 450 words. This, though, would still leave 99.8 percent of the Gospel uncorrupted. If subsequent scribes made 500 copies of Mark based on this "flawed" copy, and each one preserved all 25 mistakes, the total number of variants would now have risen to 12,500. This is more variants than words; but the variants are spread throughout 500 copies, while the text itself has still remained 99.8 percent intact. Ehrman knows this, but he continues to hype the quantity of variants as if this sounds the death knell for the reliability of Scripture.

---

[56] Komoszewski, Sawyer, and Wallace, *Reinventing Jesus*, 71.

[57] Bruce M. Metzger and Bart D. Ehrman, *The Text of the New Testament: Its Transmission, Corruption, and Restoration*, 4th edition (Oxford: Oxford University Press, 2005), 126.

[58] Metzger and Ehrman, *The Text of the New Testament*, 51.

The real issue, however, is not the number of variants, but whether they are significant enough to alter our understanding of Jesus. In nearly every single case, discrepancies between copies are due to spelling mistakes, grammatical errors, different renderings of proper names, substituting proper names in place of pronouns, and changes in word order—none of which affect the text's meaning. Admittedly, there are a handful of exceptions. The earliest copies of the Gospels have neither the account of the woman caught in adultery (John 8), for example, nor Jesus telling his disciples they can drink poison without being harmed (Mark 16). Yet even variants such as these do not jeopardize a single point of doctrine, and they pose absolutely no threat to the overall reliability of the texts. As Ehrman himself is forced to acknowledge:

> To be sure, of all the hundreds of thousands of textual changes among our [New Testament] manuscripts, most of them are completely insignificant, immaterial, and of no real importance for anything other than showing that scribes could not spell or keep focused any better than the rest of us. . . . For the most part, their intention was to conserve the tradition, not to change it.[59]

Thus, based on the nature of the variants, the number of ancient copies, and the dates for the earliest known texts, there is no basis for doubting the integrity of the Gospel manuscripts.

RELIABLE SOURCES, EARLY COMPOSITION, AND FAITHFUL PRESERVATION

Ancient historians were fully aware that the value of their reports largely depended on how their data was acquired. If they relied on sources coming long after the events, such that no living witnesses could confirm or deny what really occurred, their work was open to criticism. Hence, professionals such as Thucydides, Xenophon,

---

[59] Ehrman, *Misquoting Jesus*, 207, 215. For a scholarly guide to the variants, see Bruce M. Metzger, *A Textual Commentary on the Greek New Testament*, 2d edition (Stuttgart: Deutsche Bibelgesellschaft, 1994).

Polybius, Josephus, and Tacitus were convinced that eyewitness testimony is of paramount importance for reliable history. Not only should those who experienced the events firsthand be consulted, but the narrative should also be composed during their lifetimes.[60] If the Gospels were based on eyewitness accounts, we have an excellent basis for trusting their contents.

Ehrman is correct, however, when he says all four Gospels are anonymous.[61] As far as we know, the authors did not append their names to the original autographs; it was later scribes who added "Matthew" to one, "Mark" to another, and so forth. Ehrman speculates this happened at the end of the second century, when Christians needed to establish the authority of their texts over Gnostic Gospels which *did* bear the names of Jesus' companions (such as Thomas, Mary, and Judas).[62] Authorship for the canonical Gospels, he continues, was based on nothing more than "rumors,"[63] which has misled readers to think the texts "relate the truth of what actually happened in Jesus' life."[64] We must ask, then, whether there is still good reason to think these accounts are based on eyewitness testimony.

The earliest reference to Gospel authorship comes from Papias, a bishop following good historical methods. Around AD 80, while eyewitnesses of Jesus were still living and teaching, Papias, after making careful inquiries and relying on oral testimony, noted that Peter's oral preaching was recorded by Mark, and that Matthew himself also composed a work about Jesus. This is not mere rumor, nor is it likely that Papias gullibly accepted a tradition that "had been

---

[60] Even if the historian himself participated in the events, it was customary to interview additional witnesses for a fuller picture of what happened. See Bauckham, *Jesus and the Eyewitnesses*, 8–11.

[61] Ehrman, *Forged*, 223.

[62] On the Gnostic Gospels, see Darrell L. Bock, *The Missing Gospels: Unearthing the Truth Behind Alternative Christianities* (Nashville: Nelson Books, 2006).

[63] Ehrman, *Forged*, 226.

[64] Ehrman, *Jesus, Interrupted*, 103.

made up," as Ehrman suggests.[65] Rather, it comes from an early date and from someone who deliberately collected data from any who qualified as "a living and surviving voice."[66] This means the first and second Gospels can be tied to two of Jesus' closest disciples.

The author of the third Gospel admits that he never met Jesus in person. Accordingly, he stressed that his biography remains trustworthy because he, too, followed the practice of a faithful historian. Namely, he received information from eyewitnesses, carefully investigated everything, and wanted his audience to have certainty about what happened (Luke 1:1–4). From this author's second work, the book of Acts, we know that he was both a companion of Paul and was in Jerusalem when disciples and witnesses of Jesus, such as James, were still there (Acts 21:18).[67] This, coupled with the writer's obvious concern that his narrative be viewed as part of world history (cf. Luke 2:1–4; 3:1–2), makes him a strong candidate for having produced a reliable account.

The fourth Gospel comes closest to revealing the name of its author, but stops short by referring to him as the beloved disciple:

> Peter turned and saw the disciple whom Jesus loved following them. . . . This is the disciple who is bearing witness about these things, and who has written these things, and we know that his testimony is true. (John 21:20, 24)

Based on linguistic usage of the Greek word "has written" (*graphein*), this can only mean that the beloved disciple himself wrote the text, or that he dictated it to a scribe.[68] Either way, we have an eyewitness of

---

[65] Ehrman, *Jesus, Interrupted,* 109.

[66] Quoted in Bauckham, *Jesus and the Eyewitnesses,* 15. I am unaware of any place where Ehrman deals with Bauckham's extensive work on either Papias or the importance of eyewitness testimony.

[67] That the "we" sections of Acts are not a literary device but reflect eyewitness authorship is established by Joseph A. Fitzmyer, *Luke the Theologian: Aspects of his Teaching* (Mahwah, NJ: Paulist Press, 1989), 1–26.

[68] Bauckham, *Jesus and the Eyewitnesses,* 361.

Jesus directly responsible for this Gospel's content. Ehrman disagrees based on the distinction of "we" and "his," thinking this puts considerable distance between the author and the disciple.[69] Similarly, Ehrman criticizes all the Gospels because the authors "never speak in the first person," implying they never claimed participation in any of the events.[70] But ancient Greek authors typically referred to themselves in the third person if they were included as characters in their own narrative.[71] This is seen when the beloved disciple makes virtually the same claim regarding his vantage point at the crucifixion: "He who saw it has borne witness—his testimony is true, and he knows that he is telling the truth—that you may also believe" (John 19:35). It is only at the end, after the beloved disciple reveals himself as the author, that he switches from the third person "he" to the first person "we." The plural may sound awkward in English; but it was commonly used by ancient writers to intensify the authority expressed—somewhat like the royal "we" in English.[72] Thus, the words of John 21 should be taken at face value.

Two Gospels, Matthew and John, came directly from disciples of Jesus. The other two were written by those who had contact with eyewitnesses: the Gospel of Mark contains the words of Peter; the Gospel of Luke is based on the testimony of early Christians who knew Jesus, likely including Jesus' own relatives and certain apostles. This alone, regardless of the precise names of the authors, qualifies each Gospel as legitimate history, which would have been accepted as such by the historians of their day.

Thanks to Papias, we can say with confidence that Matthew and Mark wrote the Gospels attributed to them. For Luke and John, we do not have evidence for their authorship dating back to the first century.

---

[69] Ehrman, *Jesus, Interrupted*, 104.

[70] Ehrman, *Forged*, 228.

[71] Bauckham, *Jesus and the Eyewitnesses*, 361.

[72] Bauckham, *Jesus and the Eyewitnesses*, 369–83. Here Bauckham also discusses the import of John 1:14: "And the Word became truth and dwelt among us, and we have seen His glory."

It is not insignificant, however, that second-century Christians were unanimous as to who wrote the third Gospel—no one other than Luke was ever suggested. Nor should it be overlooked that the epistles of Paul (with whom Luke's author traveled) refer to Luke as a "beloved physician" (Colossians 4:14) and as the only one remaining with Paul as his death neared (2 Timothy 4:11). The identity of the beloved disciple has perplexed modern scholars, but the primitive church believed without difficulty that it was the apostle John.

One has to wonder why, if Ehrman is correct that names were attached to the Gospels only in response to spurious Gospels produced by heretics, Mark and Luke were selected. Since Mark was not an eyewitness but wrote down what Peter said, would not "The Gospel of Peter" have been a more compelling title? Luke is scarcely mentioned in the New Testament and would hardly have been as authoritative a name as Thomas, Philip, or Mary—names attached to the Gnostic texts. That early Christians did not fabricate authorship for the second and third Gospels, when they easily could have done so, increases the likelihood that they did not do so with the first and fourth. But again, the fact that they contain testimony from those who knew Jesus firsthand is what makes them reliable, not simply knowing the names of the authors.

A brief word must be said here about when the Gospels were written in relation to their accuracy. As mentioned above, virtually all scholars think they were written in the second half of the first century (AD 50–100). Since Jesus' crucifixion, resurrection, and ascension occurred c. 30, that means the Gospels were composed anywhere from twenty to seventy years later. While it is impossible to date any of them precisely, there are good reasons for thinking at least the synoptics date closer to the middle of the first century. If Papias is correct, for example, then Matthew and Mark existed before 80. Also, the best explanation for the last chapters of Acts including Paul's arrest and trial before Caesar, while the outcome is not given, is that Acts was finished when Paul was still awaiting his verdict.[73] Since Paul died c. 65, Acts would be dated before then, and Luke would

---

[73] Blomberg, *The Historical Reliability of the Gospels*, 29.

have been written even earlier. Many scholars also think Matthew and Luke relied on Mark for material, which would make the second Gospel earlier still.[74] Even Ehrman is willing to date Mark in the mid-60s, and Matthew and Luke in the mid-70s.[75] While this is later than some conservative scholars date them, eyewitnesses of Jesus were still living at that time—including hostile ones. The import of this point was well noted by F. F. Bruce:

> The disciples could not afford to risk inaccuracies (not to speak of willful manipulation of the facts), which would at once be exposed by those who would be only too glad to do so. . . . Had there been any tendency to depart from the facts [hostile witnesses] would have served as a further corrective.[76]

Indeed, not until the second century, when all the eyewitnesses were dead, did unbelievers produce texts that challenged what Matthew, Mark, Luke, and John reported about Jesus.

There is also the question of whether the oral tradition about Jesus would have been preserved before it was committed to writing. Three decades can sound like a long time to remember exact words and deeds and to tell and retell what happened without distortion. This is because "we are all children of Gutenberg,"[77] and fail to understand how the collection and transmission of data occurred in oral cultures. Like Ehrman, we think the child's game of "telephone" is proof enough that the passing of information quickly corrupts it.[78]

Jesus and his followers, however, lived in a culture where rabbis memorized the entire Hebrew Bible, and rote memory was the primary means of education for Jewish boys. It was not only expected

---

[74] On the relation of the Gospels to each other, see the summary in Blomberg, *The Historical Reliability of the Gospels*, 37–47.

[75] Ehrman, *Jesus*, 48.

[76] Bruce, *The New Testament Documents*, 45–46.

[77] Dunn, *A New Perspective on Jesus*, 36.

[78] Ehrman, *Jesus*, 51–52.

but also quite natural that they would memorize and retain large chunks of material. Kenneth Bailey, who studied Middle Eastern villages for over thirty years, found that the reciting of major events and their significance remained constant in oral cultures, even when material was occasionally paraphrased, rearranged, and added or deleted.[79] The tradition was controlled, in part, by a handful of key individuals who possessed a common memory of the data. This was the function of Jesus' closest disciples, verifying the message as proclaimed by others (Acts 8:14), meeting with one another to deal with disputes (Acts 15:1–11), and never inventing material that easily could have solved problems or furthered their cause.

What is more, over eighty percent of Jesus' sayings are in forms that were easy to remember (due to imagery, figures of speech, poetic phrases, etc.),[80] and his miracles were not likely to have been forgotten no matter how much time passed. Add to this the fact that he was viewed as a rabbi, a prophet, the Messiah, and the incarnate Son of God who, upon rising from the dead(!), commanded his disciples to take his teachings to the ends of the earth (Matthew 28:19), and there are excellent reasons for thinking his followers were motivated to uphold the truth. Finally, some rabbis and their followers did take shorthand notes, which may have been incorporated into the Gospels in the case of Jesus.[81] Just as the identity of the authors is not as important as whether eyewitness testimony stands behind the Gospels, the exact date of each is not as vital as whether the disciples were willing and able to preserve the tradition.

---

[79] Kenneth E. Bailey, "Informal Controlled Oral Tradition and the Synoptic Gospels," *Asia Journal of Theology* 5 (1991): 34–54.

[80] See Robert H. Stein, *The Method and Message of Jesus' Teaching*, revised edition (Louisville, KY: Westminster, 1994), 1–32.

[81] Komoszewski, Sawyer, and Wallace, *Reinventing Jesus*, 38. They also note the parallel of the Teacher of Righteousness at Qumran, whose teachings appear to have been written down before he died.

EXTERNAL EVIDENCES

That the Gospels relate genuine history becomes further apparent when considering corroborating evidence outside the texts (admitting, though, that the Gospels themselves provide superior and sufficient information about Jesus). Such evidences were not discovered for this explicit purpose, of course; scholars merely searched for the truth, letting the chips fall where they may. As ancient historian Paul Maier observes, it just so happens that "the vast percentage [of chips] fall in a manner highly congenial to the biblical record!"[82] Though there are literally thousands of them, we can only mention a handful here, including contemporary writings and archaeological finds.

Ehrman declares that if Jesus really was as important as Christians assert, "we could expect to find scores of accounts" about him, "written by contemporaries outside the group of his closest disciples." Since we supposedly do not, Ehrman concludes, "Jesus' impact on society in the first century was practically nil."[83] This is a straw man argument. Ehrman apparently limits "contemporaries" to those who were born prior to AD 30, and overlooks the fact that half the New Testament (including two of the Gospels) was written by those who were not close disciples. Based on the practice of first-century historians, it is remarkable that Jesus should be mentioned in secular accounts at all. He was from an obscure town and remained unknown for his first thirty years, belonged to a minority people, adhered to a marginal religion, and suffered the most disgraceful death possible at the hands of his own people, with even his friends abandoning him. Nevertheless, at least three non-Christian historians made reference to Jesus between AD 90 and 115.

The earliest and most famous reference comes from Josephus, from whom we learn: a) Jesus was a wise teacher; b) Jesus performed startling deeds; c) Jesus gained a following of both Jews and Greeks; d) Jesus had a brother named James; e) Jesus was called the Christ;

---

[82] Paul L. Maier, *In the Fullness of Time: A Historian Looks at Christmas, Easter, and the Early Church* (Grand Rapids: Kregel, 1997), xvii.

[83] Erhman, *Jesus*, 56.

f) leading Jews made accusation against Jesus; g) Pilate had Jesus crucified; h) Jesus' followers claimed that he rose from the dead; i) they were called Christians; j) their movement persisted in Josephus' own day.[84] Tacitus tells us the Christian movement began with "Christus," who was crucified under Pilate in Judea. Similarly, Suetonius implies Christians were a Jewish sect who followed "Chrestus." Both noted that Christians believed a "mischievous" superstition, which could be how pagans interpreted claims of a bodily resurrection.[85] All these details correspond to the texts of the Gospels.

So, too, do the plentiful artifacts already uncovered by modern archaeology, though the discipline is only about 125 years old. For the Gospels, we must limit ourselves to a few examples. The first regards Luke's infamous lines explaining why Jesus was born in Bethlehem instead of Nazareth: "In those days a decree went out from Caesar Augustus that all the world should be registered. . . . And all went to be registered, each to his own town" (Luke 2:1, 3). Not a few scholars, including Ehrman,[86] have charged Luke with inventing both the census and the Bethlehem birth as a way to spruce up Jesus' messianic credentials. (Micah 5:2 says the Messiah will come from Bethlehem, the city of his forefather, King David.) Yet two discoveries support Luke's Christmas story. Inscribed on the wall of a temple in modern-day Turkey are the "Acts of Augustus"—thirty-five deeds for which this Caesar wished to be remembered. The census of Luke 2 made eighth place on the list. There was also found a Roman census edict, which reads: "The house-to-house census having started, it is essential that all persons who for any reasons whatsoever are absent from their homes be summoned to return . . . [for]

---

[84] See *Josephus: The Essential Works*, trans. and ed. Paul L. Maier (Grand Rapids: Kregel, 1988), 269–70, 281–83.

[85] Tacitus, *Annals* 15.44; Suetonius, *Life of Claudius* 25.4; idem, *Life of Nero* 16.2.

[86] Ehrman, *Jesus*, 38–39.

registration."[87] Mary and Joseph, descendents of David, would have complied by registering in Bethlehem.

The two officials most responsible for Jesus' death, the Roman governor Pontius Pilate and the Jewish high priest Caiaphas, are both mentioned in extra-biblical writings, though nothing from archaeology confirmed their existence for years. In 1961, though, an inscription was found at Caesarea Maritima, where Pilate lived. Though some of the letters have been chipped away, his name, title, and jurisdiction are unmistakable: "Pontius Pilate, Prefect of Judea." Almost thirty years later, in 1990, a burial cave near Jerusalem was discovered containing twelve ossuaries. One was elegantly decorated, and bore the name "Caiaphas" in Aramaic; inside were the bones of a sixty-year old man.[88] Finds such as these help substantiate that the cast of characters surrounding Jesus were real people.

Finally, there is the crucifixion itself. While there is strong evidence for the site of Calvary,[89] it is the account of Jesus' slow and torturous death that has especially intrigued historians. Nowhere is a single case of crucifixion described in such detail as in the Gospels. Some have accused the writers of exaggerations or inaccuracies, but at least partial corroboration of their accounts has come from a unique discovery. In 1968, the first remains of a known crucifixion victim were found, his ankle bone still attached to a piece of his cross by an iron spike. A Jewish male, he was put to death sometime in the late 20s AD—during the reign of Pilate. Three of his four lower leg bones were broken, likely to hasten his death.[90] Here we have a very probable parallel to the criminals crucified with Jesus, as described in the Gospels. Once again, we see how archaeology can corroborate the biographies of Matthew, Mark, Luke, and John.

---

[87] Quoted in Maier, *In the Fullness of Time*, 339.

[88] See Maier, *In the Fullness of Time*, 112, 145–47.

[89] See Maier, *In the Fullness of Time*, 168–69.

[90] Craig A. Evans, "The Silence of Burial" in *Jesus, the Final Days: What Really Happened*, ed. Troy A. Miller (Louisville, KY: Westminster, 2009), 53–55.

CONCLUSION

If one begins with the premise that miracles are impossible, one can no longer examine the Gospels as an open-minded historian, but will have adopted a philosophical position inimical to evaluating facts on their own merits. And if one thinks theology and history mix about as well as oil and water, assuming that religious bias necessarily disqualifies an author, then the verdict that the Gospels are less than factual reports is unavoidable. Bart Ehrman is guilty of embracing these starting points, both of which are unwarranted. This in itself would be enough to question the rigor of his research and the reasonableness of his conclusions.

When critical scholarship has been applied to the Gospels, Ehrman has fared little better. Neither his assumption that oral traditions about Jesus were changed by anonymous, isolated communities, nor his comparison of this to folklore, is supported by the evidence. Christians communicated freely between communities in the first century; and the Gospels were written as historical biographies. Ehrman also thinks the differences between the four Gospels is evidence that each writer modified information about Jesus whenever it painted a better theological picture. But the differences are neither as great as Ehrman makes them out to be, nor are they irreconcilable when the standards of first-century historians are considered.

It is often presumed that a made-up Christ of faith was more important to early Christians than the Jesus of history, and that any theology which is "too high" must be unoriginal. This not only discounts the impact Jesus undeniably had on his followers; it also assumes nothing he said or did could have been terribly profound. Attempting to discover the real Jesus, Ehrman also twists and exploits the positive criteria of authenticity to make the Gospels appear less credible than they actually are.

The historical argument demonstrates that Matthew, Mark, Luke, and John are credible biographies of Jesus. Their manuscript evidence is far better than any other work from Greco-Roman antiquity. The amount of time between the original writings and our earliest copies is virtually negligible, and the sheer number of copies is staggering. Contrary to Ehrman, textual criticism allows us to know what the authors wrote with an amazingly high level of probability. None of the variants impact our understanding of Jesus, nor do they challenge any point of Christian doctrine.

Eyewitness testimony was relied on for each of the four Gospels. The best evidence indicates that three of Jesus' closest followers— Matthew, Peter, and the beloved disciple—stand behind the Gospels of Matthew, Mark, and John. The author of the third Gospel compensated for the fact that he never knew Jesus by consulting those who did, such as the apostles and Jesus' relatives. Significantly, narratives about Jesus were being composed when both favorable and hostile witnesses were still living and could protest any gross inaccuracies; yet no written challenges appear before the second century. Even before the Gospels, Jesus' words and deeds would have been easily remembered in an oral culture.

Verification for much of what the Gospels record comes also from external sources. Other ancient historians confirm numerous details about Jesus, especially his crucifixion under Pilate and his followers persisting in their devotion to him even after his shameful death. Archaeological finds have increased confidence in both the details and the overall narrative of the Gospels, from Jesus' birth to his death—and such support will likely increase over time.

For the person who wants to know whether the Gospels are historically reliable, the available evidence indicates they certainly are. Those who disagree generally begin from cramped starting points and with unreasonable assumptions. When the Gospels are treated as any other ancient documents purporting to record history, their trustworthy character is clearly evident.

FOR FURTHER READING

Bauckham, Richard. *Jesus and the Eyewitnesses: The Gospels as Eyewitness Testimony*. Grand Rapids: Eerdmans, 2006.

Blomberg, Craig. *The Historical Reliability of the Gospels*. 2d edition. Downers Grove, IL: InterVarsity, 2007

Evans, Craig A. *Fabricating Jesus: How Modern Scholars Distort the Gospels*. Downers Grove, IL: InterVarsity, 2006.

Habermas, Gary R. *The Historical Jesus: Ancient Evidence for the Life of Christ*. Joplin, MO: College Press, 1996.

Komoszewski, J. Ed, M. James Sawyer, and Daniel B. Wallace, eds. *Reinventing Jesus: How Contemporary Skeptics Miss the Real Jesus and Mislead Popular Culture*. Grand Rapids: Kregel, 2006.

Maier, Paul L. *In the Fullness of Time: A Historian Looks at Christmas, Easter, and the Early Church*. Grand Rapids: Kregel, 1997.

Roberts, Mark D. *Can We Trust the Gospels? Investigating the Reliability of Matthew, Mark, Luke, and John*. Wheaton, IL: Crossway, 2007.

Strobel, Lee. *The Case for the Real Jesus: A Journalist Investigates Current Attacks on the Identity of Christ*. Grand Rapids: Zondervan, 2007.

Wilkens, Michael J. and J. P. Moreland, eds. *Jesus Under Fire: Modern Scholarship Reinvents the Historical Jesus*. Grand Rapids: Zondervan, 1995.

3

THE RESURRECTION OF JESUS CHRIST ON TRIAL

EASTER TRIUMPH, EASTER LEGEND, OR EASTER FRAUD?

Craig A. Parton

LAWYERS, TRIALS, AND EVIDENCE:
INVESTIGATING THE RESURRECTION OF CHRIST

Make no mistake: if He rose at all
it was as His body;
if the cells' dissolution did not reverse, the molecules
reknit, the amino acids rekindle,
The Church will fall.

—John Updike[1]

Did you hear about the recent tragedy? A chartered bus carrying a contingent of trial lawyers went over an embankment, killing all on board. The tragedy was that there was an empty seat on the bus.

This is the way much of modern culture perceives the value of the legal profession. At best, it is a necessary evil. At worst, it is interested, like the Sophists of Plato's time, in "making the worse argument appear the better." So, why should we even care about what lawyers or the legal profession might have to say about the Christian faith? In particular, why should we care about whether lawyers have investigated the central truth claim of Christianity—i.e., the bodily resurrection of Jesus Christ from the dead—as opposed to, say, whether orthodontists have focused their analytical abilities on the resurrection? Instead of looking at how lawyers view Jesus, wouldn't it be more interesting (and vastly more entertaining) to see how Jesus viewed lawyers?

We suggest three reasons why lawyerly investigations of the resurrection should be of more than passing interest. First, lawyers, not widely considered to be naturally religious creatures, can hardly be seen as "pre-conditioned" to roll over and accept the claims of

---

[1]   "Seven Stanzas at Easter" from *Telephone Poles & Other Poems* by John Updike, copyright © 1959 by John Updike. Used by permission of Alfred A. Knopf, a division of Random house, Inc.

Christianity and, more particularly, the resurrection. Second, the law is interested in facts and evidence. Behind almost every legal dispute is a factual dispute. Every legitimate law school in the country requires a course in Evidence, virtually every Bar Exam in the country tests on the Federal Rules of Evidence, and the western common law tradition has developed sophisticated procedures and rules to determine what is reliable evidence and what standards that evidence must meet in order to be admissible for consideration by a jury. Lawyers, then, can be expected to ask what facts and evidence exist for the resurrection and won't be inclined to allow puffery to substitute for proof. Finally, trial lawyers go for verdicts. Unlike the eternal discussions of philosophers and theologians, lawsuits have finality to them.[2] And in the realm of the resurrection, a verdict is required; it either happened or it did not. Trial lawyers argue for a verdict that is founded on fact, not on mere sentiment regarding how one wishes the world were constructed.[3]

This being the case, it is worth considering the basic pillars of any trial. First, a trial is interested in getting to the facts, and so is built on evidence. Trials simply recreate history; they are largely about what happened in the past. Sometimes that history can be so ancient that living witnesses are not around to testify, for example, to the origins of a will written one hundred years ago. All the admissible evidence may be in the form of documents, with no breathing beings available to take the stand. This is the case with the resurrection of Christ; the first question is a factual one—did it happen or not?—and the extant evidence exists only in documents.

---

[2] We note that the never-ending Chancery Court case of Jarndyce v. Jarndyce in Charles Dickens' fictional *Bleak House*—in which the legal fees, after generations of haggling, consumed the entire value of the estate in dispute—was a probate matter and thus did not involve a jury trial ending in a verdict. Even current trials before the International Court of Criminal Justice at The Hague, though slated to last close to two years in some cases, do end in a judgment.

[3] As Marcel Proust noted: "Any mental activity is easy if it need not take reality into account." *The Faber Book of Aphorisms*, ed. W. H. Auden (London: Faber & Faber, 1974), 347.

Second, a trial requires that the lawyers *assume the least* and *prove the most*. So-called "presuppositions of content" are frowned upon. The strange, the fantastic, and the bizarre are daily fare in trial courts; yet the question remains, what does the evidence establish? It is not acceptable at trial to "defend" against a claim by saying, "sure, the evidence all points to that explanation, but that would mean something happened that has never happened before."

Third, the primary interests of a trial, facts and evidence, are necessarily probabilistic in nature. Unlike in the abstract realms of logic or mathematics, absolute certainty is not possible in the realm of empirical fact, as has been carefully shown by the analytic school of philosophy.[4] So the case for the resurrection, like any matter of fact, must meet criteria of admissibility such as those found in the standards of either civil or criminal law. Make no mistake: these standards are rigorous; yet absolute certainty is *never* required for a verdict, even when the very life of a defendant is on the line.

This last point is worth noting in particular, because it is critical to know what we mean when we say we can "prove" the case for Christianity—and, in particular, the case for the resurrection of Jesus. We do not mean, and necessarily cannot mean, that other "possible" explanations do not exist, and that the case is therefore one hundred percent certain. Other explanations do exist, as we shall see; none, though, is the best explanation in light of the full scope of admissible evidence. Trial lawyers are not interested in *possible* explanations of events that meet some posited criteria of rational consistency. They are instead interested in the most *probable* explanation of events that takes into consideration the maximum amount of admissible data. They understand that matters of fact never rise to the level of absolute certainty, but that such certainty pertains only to matters of pure logic

---

[4] See, e.g., A. J. Ayer, *Language, Truth and Logic* (Mineola, NY: Dover Books, 1952), as well as *Logical Positivism*, ed. A. J. Ayer (Glencoe, IL: Free Press, 1959), 69–73. For the contributions of analytical philosophy to the defense of Christianity, see John Warwick Montgomery, "Inspiration and Inerrancy: A New Departure," in *Crisis in Lutheran Theology* (Minneapolis: Bethany Books, 1967), 1:15–44.

or pure mathematics—and here only because it is built, by definition, into the system from the start.

Christianity has direct and important links to the world of trial lawyers and verdicts. Christianity is fact-centered and therefore welcomes (indeed *insists* upon) careful and thoughtful examination. It asks that the investigator make only the basic assumptions necessary to engage in the inductive process.[5] Therefore it should not be surprising that the New Testament documents do not simply announce the bodily resurrection of Jesus Christ and demand its acceptance as part of an existential "leap of faith." Instead, those documents anchor the entire legitimacy of the Christian religion on the externality and detailed facticity of the bodily resurrection of Christ and literally plead for this to be investigated.[6]

Throughout history, lawyers have recognized that if the case for the resurrection is punctured, then the Christian religion is blown apart according to the precise standard found within the very documents that present that resurrection account. Discover the body of Jesus and, very simply, the case must be dismissed; the Christian church falls. It is as simple as that, and Paul states this bluntly: if Christ is still in the grave, we are still in our sins and any belief in this man is vain superstition (1 Corinthians 15:14). Christianity, unlike virtually all of the world's other religions, is intentionally vulnerable to factual investigation.[7] It claims to be based on numerous,

---

[5] Of course all real science operates with certain basic and necessary presuppositions, such as the existence and reality of the external world, the subject-object distinction, and the meaningfulness of language to describe that external world. See, e.g., Victor F. Lenzen, *Procedures of Empirical Science* (Chicago: University of Chicago Press, 1938), 28.

[6] Paul, e.g., argues that these events did not "happen in a corner," he appeals to the many witnesses still alive, and he challenges the "jurors" to talk to *them* if they do not believe him (Acts 26:26; 1 Corinthians 15:6).

[7] Other than Judaism, only Islam and perhaps Mormonism claim to have anything approaching a serious concern for the facts of history. The various Eastern and New Age religions are not interested in verification of religious truth claims or in facts but in entering into their position in order to find self-authentication and personal fulfillment. Judaism's

sufficient, and compelling evidences—"many proofs," says Dr. Luke (Acts 1:3). That these proofs are indeed many and convincing is confirmed by the vast number of trial lawyers who have investigated and substantiated the case for the resurrection.[8] It is telling that those trained in evidence and fact finding, and who make their living in the land of verdicts, have repeatedly over the centuries put the resurrection on trial and found its defense unassailable.

We therefore look at the case for the resurrection as would be done in a trial court. Before we do so, it is critical to remember two final points. First, the burden of proof for establishing the claims of Christianity in general and the resurrection in particular are on the Christian, since he is the one asserting an affirmative case, namely, that the resurrection occurred as described in the primary source documents. Second, and as noted previously, the investigator of this evidence cannot require a standard of proof that is impossible to establish even in principle, because matters of fact always involve issues of probability. Probability reasoning, notes John Warwick Montgomery, is essentially universal in the law, operative both in common law and in non-common law systems of jurisprudence,

---

documentary trail pales in comparison to the transmissional solidity of the New Testament documents, while the factual and ethical problems within the *Koran* and the *Book of Mormon* are well documented by trial lawyers. See, e.g., J. N. D. Anderson, *The World's Religions* (Grand Rapids: Eerdmans, 1972); Sir Lionel Luckhoo, *The Quran is Not the Word of God* (Dallas: Luckhoo Ministries, n.d.); Ross Clifford, *Jesus and the Gods of the New Age* (Oxford: Lion, 2001).

[8] See Ross Clifford, *John Warwick Montgomery's Legal Apologetic: An Apologetic for All Seasons* (Bonn: Verlag für Kultur und Wissenschaft, 2004), "Appendix I: Table of Lawyers' Apologetical Writings," which lists over thirty-five trial lawyers who have analyzed the various truth claims of Christianity. For an even more detailed survey, see Philip Johnson, "Juridical Apologetics 1600–2000 A.D.: A Bio-Bibliographical Essay," *Global Journal of Classical Theology* 3 (March 2002), 1–25. Johnson's list ranges from Hugo Grotius (the "father of international law") in the 1600s to the present day with such legal apologists as John Warwick Montgomery, Sir Norman Anderson, Lord Hailsham, Gleason Archer, and Jacques Ellul.

indiscriminately in both "civilized" and "primitive" legal systems.[9] Gladly accepting the criminal standard,[10] and applying it to the question of the resurrection, we will establish that the case for the central claim of Christianity is established "beyond a reasonable doubt and to a moral certainty."[11]

Before moving to that legal case for the resurrection, it is important that we see the consequences that flow from rejecting the legal method and instead applying unique (and utterly unscholarly) standards of proof to the texts that record the resurrection of Christ. A particularly troubling example of the array of textually baseless as well as speculative opinions that one can conjure up is found in Dan Barker's influential 2008 book, *Godless: How an Evangelical Preacher Became One of America's Leading Atheists.*[12]

---

[9] John Warwick Montgomery, *Law and Gospel: A Study in Jurisprudence* (Calgary, AB: Canadian Institute for Law, Theology and Public Policy, 1995), 34–37.

[10] As for the civil standard of proof, Federal Civil Jury Instruction 72.01 defines "preponderance of the evidence" as the clear burden put upon the plaintiff in any civil action. The judge in a federal civil jury trial can instruct as follows on the issue of the burden of proof: "A preponderance of evidence in the case means such evidence as, when considered and compared with that opposed to it, has more convincing force, and produces in your minds belief that what is sought to be proved is more likely true than not true. *This rule does not, of course, require proof to an absolute certainty, since proof to an absolute certainty is seldom possible in any case*" (emphasis added).

[11] See further in John Warwick Montgomery, *Tractatus Logico-Theologicus*, 4th edition (Bonn: Verlag für Kultur und Wissenschaft, 2009), proposition three, especially paragraphs 3.61–3.78531: "Historical, jurisprudential, and scientific standards of evidence offer the touchstone for resolving the religious predicament by establishing the truth claims of Christian proclamation."

[12] Dan Barker, *Godless: How an Evangelical Preacher Became One of America's Leading Atheists* (Berkeley: Ulysses Press, 2008). The book's foreword is provided by prominent "New Atheist" Richard Dawkins, and opens with Barker discussing his appearance on the Oprah Winfrey show. Another recent example, again by a former evangelical and convert to atheism, is Robert M. Price, *The Case Against The Case for Christ: A*

Barker's critique of the resurrection is premised on his unrelentingly skeptical view of the reliability of the New Testament text. Before even reaching the issue of the resurrection, he writes that the biblical text is "unscientific, irrational, contradictory, absurd, unhistorical, uninspiring and morally unsatisfying."[13] In addition, there is "very little that can be ascertained from the four Gospels about the historic Jesus."[14] Barker then devotes over 350 pages to creating a new Jesus. He concludes that: "(1) There is no external historical confirmation for the New Testament stories;[15] (2) The New Testament stories are internally contradictory;[16] (3) There are natural

---

New Testament Scholar Refutes the Reverend Lee Strobel (Cranford, NJ: American Atheist Press, 2010). Barker, 301–2, in fact cites Price to support one of his own theories of how the resurrection legend started, and both authors have substantially similar arguments about the reliability of the New Testament Gospels.

[13] Barker, *Godless*, 40.

[14] Barker, *Godless*, 265. Curiously, Barker has no problem finding the texts reliable enough to allow any "scholar" to conclude that Jesus "was violent . . . never once spoke out against slavery . . . never lifted a finger to eradicate poverty," and thought he was part of a privileged class and was "free to take liberally from the property and work of others." See pp. 178–79 and 215.

[15] Barker is apparently unaware of Gary Habermas' superb work analyzing 39 ancient sources establishing 110 facts concerning the life, teachings, death, and resurrection of Jesus Christ. See Habermas, *Ancient Evidence for the Life of Jesus* (Nashville: Thomas Nelson, 1984).

[16] This section of *Godless* (pp. 284–89) is largely a reprise of arguments made over 200 years ago by Thomas Paine in *The Age of Reason*. Again, the author appears unaware of the legion of scholarly works thoroughly harmonizing this supposedly unassailable list of "contradictions." See basic works by J. W. Haley and William Arndt and the best hornbook on the topic by Gleason Archer, *Encyclopedia of Bible Difficulties* (Grand Rapids: Eerdmans, 1982). Though harmonizing allegedly contradictory accounts in the Gospels in particular goes back at least as far as Augustine, and continued unabated throughout church history, Barker seems to believe that he and Paine are raising never considered problems, which may explain his apparently complete unfamiliarity with scholarly treatments of each and every supposed "contradiction" raised. Paine was

explanations for the origins of the Jesus legend;[17] and (4) The miracle reports make the story unhistorical."[18]

When the question of the resurrection is finally discussed, it is not surprising that Barker's methodology yields a completely legendary Jesus. His argument assumes a corrupted late text clearly embellished by a host of secondary and non-eyewitness sources. Barker then points out that even a substantial number of "Christians" now deny the bodily resurrection.[19] He then contends that the later followers of Jesus turned what was at best a spiritual resurrection into a physical resurrection to justify their "selling all to follow Jesus,"[20] that history

---

decisively addressed in detail and refuted in contemporaneous correspondence to him from Richard Watson. In addition, Dean Edmund Bennett of the Boston University Law School dealt with Paine's objections near the end of the nineteenth century, and more recently Joseph Gudel has addressed Paine's arguments. See Richard Watson, *An Apology for the Bible in a Series of Letters Addressed to Thomas Paine* (Glasgow: J. & A. Duncan, 1796), which continues to be reprinted and is in its eighth edition now published again in 2011; Edmund Bennett, *The Four Gospels from a Lawyer's Standpoint* (New York: Houghton, Mifflin & Co., 1899); and Joseph P. Gudel, "An Examination and Critique of Thomas Paine's *Age of Reason*," *The Simon Greenleaf Law Review* 1 (1982), 75–100.

[17] The author inevitably puts higher weight on *any* explanation that is naturalistic and excludes what the actual witnesses of the events say happened So, Barker argues, it is more "natural" to believe that Jesus did not die on the cross but only "swooned," that the disciples were actually hallucinating when they thought they saw the risen Christ, that the disciples went to the wrong tomb, and that Thomas may have been crucified in place of Jesus. See Barker, *Godless*, 280–81.

[18] Barker, *Godless*, 252, where we are also told that the Gospels are "historical fiction" and that "no credible historians" take them at face value.

[19] Barker, *Godless*, 277, where he cites research showing that 30% of "born again" American Christians and one-third of the clergy of the Church of England now deny the bodily resurrection of Christ. What this has to do with whether the resurrection in fact occurred is not made clear.

[20] Barker, *Godless*, 277–78.

cannot prove a miracle,[21] that natural explanations like the swoon theory are more plausible than any "supernatural theories,"[22] that Paul's testimony precedes that of the Gospel writers and contradicts those writers at every turn on the topic of the resurrection,[23] that Peter probably is the impetus for the "He is risen" tale that only evolved after decades of telling the Jesus story around the campfire to followers,[24] but that there is no need to become distraught because a

---

[21] In what may be news to trained historians and trial lawyers alike, Barker, 279, claims that "[h]istory is limited; it can only confirm events that conform to natural regularity." In the law, however, the standard of proof does not depend on the frequency of the event (since *all* historical events, including those at the center of trials, are unique) or on the characterization of those events as either "miraculous" or "non-miraculous." In *every* instance, the standard of proof depends on the quality of the evidence presented on behalf of the claimed event—that and *nothing more*; that and *nothing less*.

[22] Here, 279–80, Barker cites David Hume and Thomas Paine, along with Hugh Schonfield's *The Passover Plot*, discussed below.

[23] Barker argues that Paul has no angelic messages, no mourning women, no earthquakes, no bodily ascension, and most importantly, no empty tomb (affirming the resurrection of Christ apparently does not infer an empty tomb, which N. T. Wright notes is like saying that one needs to amplify the statement, "I walked down the street," with the qualification that it was "on my feet." N. T. Wright, *The Resurrection of the Son of God* [Minneapolis: Fortress Press, 2003], 321). Paul's Jesus is a mere "disembodied spirit." See Barker, *Godless*, 264 and 292–94. The conclusion Barker draws is apparently that 1 Corinthians 15 is a reliable text only in so far as it is potentially useful to drive a wedge between Paul and the Gospel writers.

[24] This theory is attributed to Robert Price and argues as follows: Peter felt remorse about denying Christ. While probably praying for forgiveness, Peter thought he heard a voice saying he was forgiven, and immediately ran into town and announced that the Lord had spoken to him. That story eventually became more than just that Jesus spoke with Peter, but that Jesus personally *appeared* to Peter. This was all very comforting to the followers of Jesus since they had given away all to follow what to that point looked like a doomed venture. Barker, *Godless*, 302. It apparently never occurs to Barker that there is no textual support whatsoever for *any* of these speculative opinions.

legendary or mythical Jesus is actually more honoring to the Gospel writers (whoever they were).[25]

We will reference Barker's position at points only to establish that the legal method is at *complete odds* with both his methodology and his conclusions because the law emphasizes fact over speculation, probability over possibility, and the real world over the kind of mythical world created by Barker.

BEFORE GETTING TO THE FLESH AND BLOOD OF THE MATTER

The assertion of the bodily resurrection of Jesus Christ is, of course, presented in the New Testament materials. Elsewhere in this volume the case for the total reliability of those primary source documents has been made and so need not be repeated here. Trial lawyers also have made the case for the reliability of the canonical Gospels as primary source documents,[26] and the solidity of those materials (i.e., what we have is what the writers wrote and that they had every means, motive, and opportunity to get the facts right) is simply beyond serious dispute. As Montgomery, himself a lawyer, notes: "To express skepticism concerning the resultant text of the New Testament books . . . is to allow all of classical antiquity to slip into obscurity, for no documents of the ancient period are as well attested bibliographically as is the New Testament."[27]

---

[25] The legend idea is "respectful to the humanity of the early Christians . . . respectful to the historical method . . . respectful to theology . . . and respectful of the freedom to believe." Barker, *Godless*, 303–4.

[26] See, e.g., those listed in Clifford, *John Warwick Montgomery's Legal Apologetic*, "Appendix I."

[27] John Warwick Montgomery, *Where is History Going? A Christian Response to Secular Philosophies of History* (Minneapolis: Bethany Books, 1969), 46; see also Craig Parton, *The Defense Never Rests* (St. Louis: Concordia, 2003), 73–86. Contrast this with Barker's misunderstanding of the importance of the number of copies and early dating of the Gospel materials as establishing their authenticity. Barker, *Godless*, 263. He confuses authenticity with truth questions and does not

The resurrection is presented by the apostolic band as the heart of their case. As we have noted, the entire verifiability of the Christian position hinges on the facticity of the resurrection. Jesus himself pinned all his claims on the factual verification that his resurrection would provide to the serious inquirer (see Matthew 12:38–40 and 16:4; Luke 11:29; John 2:18–22). But did the resurrection occur in a way that can even be verified, or is it simply to be accepted on "faith"? Initially, we must deal with the objection that a resurrection is a supernatural miracle that has been shown to be both philosophically impossible (as argued by the Scottish philosopher David Hume) and scientifically dismissible (as argued with reference to Einsteinian physics).[28]

Hume's argument against the miraculous, as C. S. Lewis rightly points out, proceeds on the belief that the need to investigate the factual case for the resurrection in particular could be eliminated simply by presenting a philosophical argument against the miraculous in general. Hume reasoned from the initial premise (generally abandoned, coincidentally, since the rise of the Einsteinian physics to which other skeptics appeal) that "a firm and unalterable experience has established these laws [of nature]." Lewis demonstrates that this premise led Hume to the entirely circular conclusion that "[t]here must, therefore, be a uniform experience against every miraculous event" and, "that a dead man should come to life has never been observed in any age or country."[29] However, there is no way of determining *a priori* whether a resurrection has occurred; instead, one

---

understand that the bibliographical argument for the authenticity of the Gospel records seeks only to prove that the text has reliably come down to us as written.

[28] These same arguments appear in Barker, *Godless*, 269–70 and 278–79.

[29] David Hume, *An Inquiry Concerning Human Understanding,* ed. C. W. Hendel (New York: Bobbs-Merrill, 1955), 122 [sec. 10 ("Of Miracles"), pt. 1]. The most accessible refutation of Hume remains C. S. Lewis, *Miracles* (New York: MacMillan, 1947); see especially chapters 8 and 13. For a more recent and utter decimation of Hume's argument, see John Earman, *Hume's Abject Failure: The Argument Against Miracles* (New York: Oxford University Press, 2000).

must *a posteriori* check out the evidence. Hume allowed eighteenth-century rationalists to sit back in their easy chairs and dismiss evidence for the resurrection without so much as lifting a finger to investigate the claim inductively. On Hume's circular reasoning, checking out evidence became intellectually unnecessary.

An even bolder move is made by those who claim, sometimes with reference to the Einsteinian theories superseding Hume's Newtonian assumptions, that no "single contrary experience" can suffice to falsify an otherwise coherent theory.[30] So, for example, even strong evidence for a "violation" of physical laws—such as a resurrection—need not require abandoning prejudices against the miraculous. Yet, it is especially in the wake of Einstein's work that "laws of nature" have increasingly been recognized not as prescriptive rules dictating what can or cannot happen in the physical world (a reflection of eighteenth-century commitments to logical consistency and deductive systems of order), but rather more modestly as simple descriptions, based on empirical observation, of what does happen.[31] Precisely this view is required by the fact that no one has a pipeline into the ultimate nature of the universe such that he knows, without checking out the actual evidence, what is "reasonable" in terms of events. Indeed, as Einstein himself remarked, "a single experiment can prove me wrong."[32]

A resurrection may not have occurred since that day in first-century Palestine, but the fact that it has not been repeated has no bearing on whether it *in fact* took place once in history. The assertion of Christ's resurrection is an historical claim and, as such, it must be investigated inductively and not dismissed (as by Barker) on the basis

---

[30] See, e.g., W. V. Quine, *From a Logical Point of View* (Cambridge: Harvard University Press, 1953), 42–43.

[31] See Karl Popper, *The Logic of Scientific Discovery* (New York: Basic Books, 1959), esp. 49–56. Also see John Warwick Montgomery, *The Shape of the Past*, rev. edition (Minneapolis: Bethany Books, 1975), 289–93.

[32] Alice Calaprice, ed., *The New Quotable Einstein* (Princeton: Princeton University Press, 2005), 291.

of thoroughly discredited philosophical reasoning based on an arrogant presumption that one knows what is "reasonable" before, and without, investigating the evidence.

DEAD MAN WALKIN': THE PESKY DETAIL OF THE MISSING BODY

We have now come to the central question of the death and resurrection of Jesus. We have seen already in this volume that the historical records containing the recitation of these events are in singularly magnificent literary shape. Further, the eyewitness accounts had the benefit of circulating amongst hostile witnesses who had every resource, motive, and opportunity to refute the claim; that is, the testimony circulated in an atmosphere effectively constituting what the law deems "cross examination." The contemporaneous written record in refutation of the resurrection is profoundly and hauntingly silent.[33] Resorting to arguments found in non-eyewitness accounts arising half a century or more later would be rejected in any court of law on the basis of hearsay and lack of foundation, especially when contradicting the primary sources of Matthew, Mark, Luke, and John. Barker, on the other hand, assumes that *any* later text (as long

---

[33] The law of evidence provides that if a party has the means to marshal contradictory evidence and fails to do so, the jury may conclude that no contradictory evidence exists. See California Evidence Code sections 412 and 413 ("Failure to explain or deny unfavorable evidence may suggest that the evidence is true." California Form of Jury Instruction, No. 205[1]). Clearly, the nascent Christian church could easily have been eliminated by the simple production of the body of Jesus. If he did not in fact rise from the dead, the Roman and Jewish leaders were clearly motivated and powerful enough to find and produce the body. (This also refutes the strange objection that the women went to the wrong, and therefore empty, tomb on Easter morning.) The argument that Jesus' followers hid the body is absurd and legally uncompelling, for they then would have suffered death for what they *knew* was a lie.

as it is *not* Matthew, Mark, Luke or John) gives more reliable information about the historical Jesus.[34]

The fact is that the evidence for the death and resurrection of Jesus Christ is as complete and as sound as any fact of the ancient world. The crucifixion of Jesus lines up precisely with what we know of first-century Roman practices. Centurions knew their business, and the eyewitness accounts perfectly describe standard Roman procedure. Thus, various detailed forensic and medical investigations of this procedure and its inevitable effects reach exactly the same conclusion: this man was dead on the cross.[35]

The issue of the missing body is therefore one of great force, and the fact of the empty tomb has been sufficient on its own merits to bring skeptics to Christian faith. Frank Morrison, for example, famously attributed his conversion to Christianity to this singular fact. Morrison reasoned that if Jesus did not rise from the dead, then only three interest groups might be suspected of removing the body: the Romans, the Jewish religious leaders, and the disciples. Yet, he noted, the Romans above all craved peace and order; the last thing they wanted was controversy. The Jewish authorities had every motivation to preserve their religious influence and control. And the disciples

---

[34] Barker, *Godless*, 252: "The Jesus of history is not the Jesus of the New Testament." One wonders if Barker understands there are no earlier, let alone better, texts than the New Testament materials on which to base the "Jesus of history."

[35] See, e.g., William D. Edwards, M.D., et al. "The Physical Death of Jesus Christ," *The Journal of the American Medical Association* 255, no. 11 (March 21, 1986), 1455–63; C. Truman Davis, M.D., "The Crucifixion of Jesus: The Passion of Christ from a Medical Point of View," *Arizona Medicine* 22 (March 1965), 183–87; James H. Jewell, Jr., M.D. and Patricia A. Didden, M.D., "A Surgeon Looks at the Cross," *Voice* 58, no. 2 (March–April 1979), 3–5. For probably the most complete analysis of crucifixion from the medical standpoint, though, see Frederick T. Zugibe, M.D., Ph.D., *The Crucifixion of Jesus: A Forensic Inquiry* (New York: M. Evans & Co., 2005). The author even recreated aspects of the crucifixion, using willing subjects in his laboratory.

would hardly steal the body, declare it raised, and then die for what they knew to be a lie.[36]

But, the skeptic might respond, works such as Hugh Schonfield's *The Passover Plot* (cited by Barker as presenting a plausible naturalistic theory) and Erich von Daniken's *Chariots of the Gods* have established alternative possible explanations of the resurrection story.[37] Since we have already outlined the legal principles of the "burden of proof" and "probabilistic reasoning," we may apply these rules to such alternative explanations. Schonfield argues that Joseph of Arimathea and Lazarus were co-conspirators who colluded with Jesus to orchestrate his own crucifixion, pass out on the cross—thus confounding the Roman guards, who assumed he was dead—and then to revive and fool the disciples into thinking he had been resurrected.[38] The novel theory proposed by von Daniken is that Jesus was the cosmic equivalent of a Martian who had otherworldly powers, making it appear that he had resurrected.

---

[36] Frank Morrison, *Who Moved the Stone? The Evidence for the Resurrection* (New York: Barnes & Noble, 1963). Morrison began looking at the resurrection as a skeptic, with the intent of debunking Christianity, but in the process became a Christian. The title of chapter one says it all: "The Book That Refused to Be Written." See also Norman Geisler, *The Battle for the Resurrection* (Nashville: Thomas Nelson, 1989), where Geisler deals with several objections to the bodily resurrection of Christ raised by everyone from liberal theologians to New Agers.

[37] Hugh Schonfield, *The Passover Plot* (New York: Bantam Books, 1981); Erich von Daniken, *Chariots of the Gods: Unsolved Mysteries of the Past* (New York: G. P. Putnam & Sons, 1969).

[38] Note that this theory does not answer how it might square with Christ's own teaching about honesty and truth-telling. See the devastating critique of Schonfield by Edwin M. Yamauchi, "Passover Plot or Easter Triumph? A Critical Review of H. Schonfield's Recent Theory," in *Christianity for the Tough-Minded,* ed. John Warwick Montgomery (Minneapolis: Bethany Books, 1973), 261–71.

What can be said about such proposed speculative possibilities, a litany of which Barker enumerates?[39] Though von Daniken himself would be subject to character impeachment based on his convictions for embezzlement, fraud, and forgery in Switzerland, we need not dismiss such theories on the basis of their originators' character.[40] These proposals are based on mere possibilities; but virtually anything is possible. Courts, however are interested in probabilities based on evidence, not theories based on mere speculation.[41]

A word must also be said about the objection to the resurrection posed by the formerly atheistic philosopher Antony Flew.[42] Flew argued that Christians simply prefer a biological miracle (i.e., Christ's resurrection from the dead) to a psychological miracle (i.e., the disciples dying for what they knew to be false). But as we have noted, the issue is not what "preference" a person has for the evidence. The question is which interpretation of the evidence considers the

---

[39] Among the "natural and thus more plausible explanations" offered by Barker are: the swoon theory, that the women went to the wrong tomb, that Peter merely heard an inner voice and that the church then created a resurrected Jesus, and that Thomas died in place of Jesus. Barker, *Godless*, 280–81.

[40] Richard R. Lingeman, "Eric von Daniken's Genesis," *New York Times Book Review* (31 March 1974), 6, writes that von Daniken had "obtained the money [more than $130,000 in debts] by misrepresentation of his financial situation, falsifying the hotel's books to make it appear solvent. A court psychiatrist examined von Daniken and found him a prestige-seeker, a liar and an unstable and criminal psychopath with a hysterical character, yet fully accountable for his acts."

[41] For a discussion of Federal Rule of Evidence 401, addressing the question of "relevant evidence," see John Warwick Montgomery, *Human Rights and Human Dignity* (Dallas: Probe Books, 1986), 153.

[42] Flew moved from atheism to a self-described "deism" on the basis of the evidence for the intelligent design of the universe. See Antony Flew and Gary Habermas, "My Pilgrimage from Atheism to Theism: A Discussion between Antony Flew and Gary Habermas," *Philosophia Christi* 6 (2004), 197–211, as well as Antony Flew and R. A. Varghese, *There is a God: How the World's Most Notorious Atheist Changed His Mind* (New York: HarperCollins, 2007).

maximum amount of factual data. If multiple eyewitness accounts have Jesus dead at point A and alive again at point B, then a resurrection, by definition, has occurred. The "deluded disciples" argument is untenable under the canons of evidence employed in a court of law; there are simply too many facts that refute the position.[43]

Similarly, any notion that the same witnesses who attest to the crucifixion and death of Jesus, and then to his appearance to them alive three days later, were seeing ghosts, or were subject to delusional visions is utterly untenable. Christ's bodily and fleshly resurrection admits no "ghost" imagery. He ate fish, walked along a road with his disciples, and offered his pierced side to Thomas for personal and tactile verification. Likewise, psychiatric research makes clear that mass delusion occurs only over highly unstable and short periods of time.[44] In the case of the witnesses of the risen Jesus after his crucifixion, the evidence against mass delusional hysteria could not be more secure. The appearances occur with a variety of people, over widely varying geographical and physical conditions, last over a month, and involve personalities hardly susceptible to ecstatic visions.[45] Many of the eyewitnesses to the resurrected Christ would suffer the most repulsive and disgusting deaths for their convictions, and so had every motivation to get the facts right.

And facts they had, not merely legends or myths. Indeed, this resurrection was decidedly *not* like those of the Greek and Persian

---

[43] See Gary Habermas and Antony Flew, *Did Jesus Rise From the Dead? The Resurrection Debate,* ed. Terry L. Miethe (San Francisco: Harper & Row, 1987); see also John Warwick Montgomery, "Science, Theology, and the Miraculous," in his *Faith Founded on Fact* (Nashville: Thomas Nelson Publishers, 1978), 43–73, esp. at 54.

[44] Paul Hoch and Joseph Zubin, eds., *Psychopathology of Perception* (New York: Grune & Stratton, 1965), 18; Paul William Preu, M.D., *Outline of Psychiatric Case-Study: A Practical Handbook* (New York: Paul Hoeber, 1939), 97–99.

[45] J. N. D. Anderson, *The Evidence for the Resurrection* (Downers Grove, IL: InterVarsity, 1966), 20–23.

myths cited by Barker.[46] The Harvard classical scholar Clifford Moore, like C. S. Lewis, knew the proper distinction between fact and myth:

> Christianity knew its Savior and Redeemer not as some god whose history was contained in a mythical faith, with rude, primitive, and even offensive elements, as were the stories of Attis, Osiris and to a degree of Dionysus. Such myths required violent interpretation to make them acceptable to enlightened minds. On the contrary, the Christian Savior had lived and associated with men whose minds and senses had apprehended his person, acts, and character. These witnesses had transmitted their knowledge directly, and they had testified to the life of Jesus Christ and his teaching. Jesus was then a historical, not a mythical being. No remote or foul myth obtruded itself on the Christian believer; his faith was founded on positive, historical and acceptable facts.[47]

BUT WHAT DOES THE RESURRECTION *MEAN*?

Critics such as Barker still respond, isn't the resurrection just another miracle (like the "healings" performed by the surgically-enhanced and well-coifed Mr. and Mrs. Televangelist) that can be easily explained in naturalistic terms?[48] Hardly. As the existentialist philosophers and analytical psychologists have been quick to point out, death is the ultimate leveler of us all. We all fear death in some sense, and so the funeral, for instance, becomes an ancient effort to help the surviving community come to grips with the devastation and seeming irrationality of death. In light of such realizations, Carl

---

[46] Barker, *Godless*, 268–70. In refutation, see Gary R. Habermas, "Resurrection Claims in Non-Christian Religions," *Religious Studies* 25 (1989), 167–77.

[47] Clifford Herschel Moore, *The Religious Thought of the Greeks* (Cambridge: Harvard University Press, 1925), 357. See also C. S. Lewis, *Surprised by Joy* (London: Geoffrey Bles, 1955), 222.

[48] Barker, *Godless*, 280–81.

Gustav Jung and Mircea Eliade, for example, convincingly argue that images associated with death are cross-cultural and indeed are "archetypes" of the collective human unconsciousness. [49]

The suggestive point here is that if God were indeed to become man and to give us insight into one issue, it would be the enigma of death. In Jesus Christ we find the announcement that, though we have brought about our own doom by our cosmic rebellion against God, God himself has acted to effect a reconciliation wholly incapable of being effected by sinful man. Jesus claimed that he had come to earth to deal with man's sin and to give a final answer to death for all who believe. If ever there was a basis for worship, it is here. Instead of coming to earth to engage trivial concerns (curing hangnails, for example, or presenting the glories of a particularly effective weight-loss program), the eternal *Logos* in the womb of the virgin became fully human to deal with the fundamental questions of human existence: Why do we die, and what follows death?

Finally, if we are presented with a choice of whose trial testimony is most competent to illuminate the meaning of the resurrection—that of Jesus, or that of his contemporary critics—we suggest it is infinitely more reasonable to accept the testimony of the one who actually accomplished his own resurrection.[50] And his confident testimony regarding the proper interpretation of his resurrection is that it establishes his deity (see John 10:30 and 14:8–9; Mark 2:5–7 and 14:61–64). Until critics like Barker accomplish their own

---

[49] Jung's discussion of the cross as an archetype is especially fascinating, even though Jung ended up holding to the position that religious belief was an entirely arbitrary and subjective decision. See Carl Gustav Jung, *Man and His Symbols* (New York: Doubleday, 1964); see also Mircea Eliade *Images & Symbols: Studies in Religious Symbolism* (New York: Sheed & Ward, 1969).

[50] For a fuller treatment of the role of law in addressing these hermeneutical issues, see Craig Parton, "A Lawyer Amongst the Theologians: Justice Scalia's Solution to Our Present Hermeneutical Chaos," in *Theologia et Apologia: Essays in Reformation Theology and its Defense*, ed. Adam S. Francisco, Korey D. Maas, and Steven P. Mueller (Eugene, OR: Wipf & Stock, 2007), 269–80.

resurrections, the testimony of the one who did remains what lawyers call the "best evidence."

Jesus himself claims that he is the center of all of Holy Writ and that to miss him as center and circumference of the whole Bible is to end in misery (see John 5:39; 14; 16; Luke 24:44).[51] This is most clearly seen when the Apostle Peter suggested that there were a variety of interpretations and "dissenting opinions" as to Christ's true identity (Matthew 16:14). But Jesus' response—"But who do *you* say that I am?" (v. 15, emphasis added)—brought the discussion down to the critical question, and to the personal, eternal consequences of the answer.

In many matters, having the "right interpretation" is of little consequence. Differing interpretations of a work by Melville, Faulkner, or Graham Greene make for interesting discussion in class, but the disagreements are hardly eternal in their ramifications. In some fields, however, getting *the* right interpretation is literally a matter of life and death. Postmodern interpretive approaches are not found, for example, amongst cancer specialists interpreting the radiological scans of their patients. Similarly, juries reach verdicts and send defendants to an appointment with a last meal and a lethal injection convinced that they have arrived at the one correct interpretation of the facts in a case.

In the same vein, we suggest that the interpretation arrived at by Peter—in his confession before Christ's death, but most consistently and forcefully in his proclamations after Christ's resurrection—has weighty consequences. Christianity rests solely on the person and work of Jesus Christ as its foundation; thus the correct understanding of these is a matter of both earthly and eternal importance.

---

[51] See also Robert P. Lightner, *The Savior and the Scriptures* (Philadelphia: Presbyterian & Reformed, 1966), and David P. Scaer, "All Theology is Christology," *Modern Reformation* 8/5 (September–October 1999), 28–32.

WHERE DOES THIS LEAVE US?

The resurrection is proclaimed in the primary source documents as of fundamental importance, as the center of apostolic preaching, and the center of the entire Gospel (see Acts 2, 4, 10, 13, and 17). Paul summarizes the substance of the Gospel by saying that "Christ died for our sins ... [and] that he was raised on the third day" (1 Corinthians 15:1–3). The Apostle goes on to say that "if you confess with your mouth that Jesus is Lord and believe in your heart that God raised him from the dead, you will be saved" (Romans 10:9).[52]

So critical is the bodily resurrection of Christ, Paul insists that if Christ did not rise from the dead, the apostles are false witnesses, the apostolic preaching is fraudulent, the Christian faith is deeply deceptive, we are all still in our sins, and that the dead in Christ are lost (see 1 Corinthians 15:14–19). The doctrine of the resurrection is so central to Christianity that any teaching that in any way denies the physical, bodily resurrection of Jesus Christ may be many things, but one thing it is not and cannot be is Christian.

Maturity means aligning one's life and beliefs with the way the world in fact is, rather than with how one hopes or wishes the world might be. The evidence for the bodily resurrection of Jesus is as solid as any fact in the ancient world. We should not be shocked that God's entrance into human history and that his victory over death and hell should be extraordinary and unusual, even miraculous. To reject this *evangelion*, or "good news," leads only, as J. R. R. Tolkien says, to "sadness or to wrath."[53]

---

[52] Barker's ultimate conclusions about sin and the need for a substitutionary atonement are hardly surprising: "It does no good to say that Jesus died on the cross to pay for our sins. I don't have any sins." Barker, *Godless*, 202.

[53] J. R. R. Tolkien, *On Fairy Stories: Essays Presented to Charles Williams* (London: Oxford University Press, 1947), 83–84.

The Apostle John, an eyewitness to the crucified and resurrected Christ,[54] records Jesus' testimony concerning the meaning of his resurrection from the dead: "I am the resurrection and the life. Whoever believes in me, though he die, yet shall he live, and everyone who lives and believes in me shall never die. Do you believe this?" (John 11:25–26). For the trial lawyers who have carefully investigated the admissible evidence for the resurrection, the only defensible answer to Jesus' request for a personal verdict is a resounding yes.[55]

FOR FURTHER READING

Bennett, Edmund. *The Four Gospels from a Lawyer's Standpoint.* Boston: Houghton, Mifflin, 1899, photolithographically reproduced with editorial introduction by John Warwick Montgomery in *The Simon Greenleaf Law Review* 1 (1981–82): 15–74.

Clifford, Ross. *Leading Lawyers' Case for the Resurrection.* Calgary, Alberta, Canada: Canadian Institute for Law, Theology and Public Policy, 1996.

---

[54] Barker asserts that the Jesus of John is a "different character" altogether from the Jesus of the synoptic Gospels. Barker's methodology, of course, requires that he draw this conclusion because his theory is that as the last Gospel writer, John was the ultimate embellisher of the Jesus legend. Barker, *Godless*, 265.

[55] Barker offers the following as a revealing view of the evidence that would convince him that Christianity was true: "If you were to tell me that God predicted to you that next March 14 at 2:27 a.m. a meteorite composed of 82 percent iron, 13 percent nickel and 3 percent iridium, approaching from the southwest and hitting the Earth at an angle of 82 degrees, would strike your house . . . , penetrating the building, punching a hole through your Navajo rug upstairs and the arm of the couch downstairs, ending up 17.4 inches below the basement floor and weighing 13.5 ounces, and if that happened as predicted, I would take that as serious evidence that atheism is falsified. If Jesus would materialize in front of a debate audience, captured on videotape, and if he were to tell us exactly where to dig in Israel to find the ark of the covenant containing the original stone tablets given to Moses—well, you get the idea." Barker, *Godless*, 75–76.

Greenleaf, Simon. *The Testimony of the Evangelists: The Gospels Examined by the Rules of Evidence.* Grand Rapids: Kregel, 1995.

Habermas, Gary, and Antony Flew. *Did Jesus Rise from the Dead? The Resurrection Debate.* San Francisco: Harper & Row, 1987.

Habermas, G. R. and M. R. Licona. *The Case for the Resurrection of Jesus.* Grand Rapids: Kregel, 2004.

Lamb, Francis. *Bible Miracles Examined by the Methods, Rules and Tests of the Science of Jurisprudence as Administered Today in Courts of Justice.* Oberlin, Ohio: Bibliotheca Sacra Company, 1909.

Licona, Michael R. *The Resurrection of Jesus: A New Historiographical Approach.* Downers Grove, IL: InterVarsity, 2010.

Moen, John T. "A Lawyer's Logical and Syllogistic Look at the Facts of the Resurrection," *Simon Greenleaf Law Review* 8 (1987–88): 81–110.

Montgomery, John Warwick. *Christ Our Advocate: Studies in Polemical Theology, Jurisprudence and Canon Law.* Bonn, Germany: Verlag für Kultur und Wissenschaft, 2002.

_____. *Law and Gospel: A Study in Jurisprudence*, 2d edition. Calgary, AB, Canada: Canadian Institute for Law, Theology and Public Policy, 1995.

Morrison, Charles Robert. *The Proofs of Christ's Resurrection: From a Lawyer's Standpoint.* Andover: Warren F. Draper, 1882.

Parton, Craig. *Religion on Trial.* Eugene, OR: Wipf & Stock, 2008.

Sherlock, Thomas. *The Tryal of the Witnesses of the Resurrection of Jesus.* London: J. Roberts, 1729, photolithographically reproduced in John Warwick Montgomery's *Jurisprudence: A Book of Readings.* Strasbourg: International Scholarly Publishers, 1980.

Swinburne, Richard. *The Resurrection of God Incarnate*. Oxford: Clarendon Press, 2003.

Wright, N. T. *The Resurrection of the Son of God*. Minneapolis: Fortress Press, 2003.

4

DEFENDING THE DEITY OF JESUS IN THE FACE OF ISLAM

Adam S. Francisco

ISLAM ON CHRISTIANITY

Before the turn of the century, Islam was rarely a topic of conversation. Today, a decade after the horrifying events of September 11, 2001, it remains at or near the top of concerns both in America and internationally. The reasons for this are numerous. The threat of future terrorist attacks, the failure of policy makers to identify their ideological roots, and the advance of Islamic causes in public space by Muslim advocacy groups are but a few. For the Christian, there is also a theological concern. Like any other non-Christian religion, Islam is antithetical to the Gospel. In fact, it strikes at the heart of the Christian confession that God was in Christ reconciling the world unto himself (2 Corinthians 5:19). The Qur'an claims, without any equivocation, that God does not have a son and that those who claim such a thing are guilty of an egregious error (19:89–90). Jesus, according to the Qur'an, was only a human messenger of God (*Allah*) and certainly not one of the divine persons of the Trinity (4:171). Asserting anything beyond this elevates a mere creature to the status of divinity (*shirk*) and is therefore, as Qur'an 9:30 puts it, anathema.

Interestingly, there are passages in the Qur'an that suggest the similarity of Christianity and Islam. Qur'an 29:46 even instructs Muslims to treat Christians kindly, since both religions, Muhammad claimed, believe in the same revelation and worship the same God.[1] Such passages as noted above, and others, raise an important question

---

[1] Qur'an 29:46: "Argue only in the best way with the People of the Book. . . . Say, 'We believe in what was revealed to us and in what was revealed to you' our god and your God are one.'" Unless contexts suggests otherwise, in the Qur'an "People of the Book" (*ahl al-kitab*) refers to both Jews and Christians. Qur'anic quotations are from the translation of M. A. S. Abdel Haleem, *The Qur'an: A New Translation* (New York: Oxford University Press, 2004). By permission of Oxford University Press.

for understanding how Muslims think about Christianity.[2] On the one hand, the Qur'an regards the two religions as essentially equal, even referring to Christians as "the nearest in affection" to Muslims. On the other, the Qur'an condemns Christianity for its confession of the deity of Jesus. How is this contradiction reconciled? Islamic legal tradition appeals to what is called the principle of abrogation (*naskh*), whereby revelations dated to the latter part of Muhammad's life are understood to have superseded earlier ones. So, for example, traditional Islamic jurisprudence takes passages such as Qur'an 9:5 and 9:29—with their injunctions to fight non-Muslims (including Christians) for rejecting Islam—as definitive.[3] The theological tradition of Islam, however, explains the contradiction differently. Referring to what seem like two contradictory views of Christianity, Syed Muhammad Naquib al-Attas notes that this apparent contradiction is due to the fact that the Qur'an knows of "two Christianities: the original and true one and the Western version of it. Original and true Christianity conformed with Islam."[4] The original and true Christianity praised by the Qur'an is no longer extant, however, except where it has been preserved in various heresies (Unitarianism, for example, or, at an earlier date, Arianism).[5] That which an orthodox Christian would regard as biblical Christianity, conversely, is denounced in the Qur'an and regarded by Muslims as a religion that was once grounded in God's revelation through his prophets, but which has, through the centuries, been corrupted by theological innovation.

---

[2] For a good cross section of Muslim views on Christianity, see Paul J. Griffiths, ed., *Christianity through Non-Christian Eyes* (Maryknoll: Orbis, 1990), 67–134.

[3] See, for example, Sayyid Qutb, *In the Shade of the Qur'an*, vol. 9, trans. Adil Salahi (Leicestershire: The Islamic Foundation, 2003), 101–2.

[4] Syed Muhammad Naquib al-Attas, *Islam and Secularism* (Kuala Lumpur: International Institute of Islamic Thought and Civilization, 1993), 20.

[5] For a Muslim view on the survival of what is regarded as original (and legitimate) Christianity, see Muhammad Ata ur-Rahim, *Jesus, Prophet of Islam* (Tahrike Tarsile Qur'an, 2000).

This belief that historic Christianity is an innovation is one of the most basic assumptions Muslims make about Christianity. It became standardized and asserted as a matter of fact in the Islamic polemical tradition by the eleventh century when the first Muslim-authored history of Christianity was produced, and was expressed two centuries later by none other than the celebrated Sheykh of Islam, Ibn Taymiyya (1263–1328), in the following words: "[T]he false religion of Christians is nothing but an innovated religion which they invented after the time of Christ and by which they changed the religion of Christ."[6] Assertions such as this certainly help Muslim apologists in explaining the veracity of Islam vis-à-vis Christianity. The problem, however, is that there is no concrete evidence of a theological conspiracy resulting in the divinization of a human prophet named Jesus, who preached essentially the same message as Islam. Even so, Muslim apologists continue to advance these claims. In fact, in recent years there has been a noticeable turn towards fact-based approaches among Muslim apologists and polemicists that, on their face, look more like serious historical arguments.

A CONTEMPORARY MUSLIM POLEMIC

Perhaps the most prolific example of this is the work of the Iraqi-born Christian turned Muslim, Louay Fatoohi. To date he has written four books on the person of Jesus, the first and most comprehensive entitled *The Mystery of the Historical Jesus*. In brief, it argues that all evidence for the Jesus of history corresponds most closely to the Jesus described in the Qur'an, and certainly not to the Christian understanding of Jesus. Fatoohi claims that Jesus was born to a woman (a virgin) named Mary, endowed with supernatural gifts, tasked by God to be one of his prophetic messengers, and even honored with the title "the Christ" (*al-Masih*). He further claims,

---

[6] Thomas Michel, *A Muslim Theologian's Response to Christianity: Ibn Taymiyya's Al-Jawab Al-Sahih* (Delmar: Caravan Books, 1984), 143. For the first Muslim history of Christianity, see the recently translated 'Abd al-Jabbar, *Critique of Christian Origins*, trans. Gabriel Said Reynolds and Samir Khalil Samir (Provo: Brigham Young University Press, 2010).

however, that Jesus was spared crucifixion through supernatural intervention, and at some point ascended into heaven; there he awaits the judgment day when he will return and, among other things, denounce Christians for ascribing to him divinity.[7]

Fatoohi's argument (and most Muslim apologetics more generally), at first, seems absurd. For what he has ostensibly done is simply preferred the traditional Muslim view of Jesus, which is based on the Qur'an—a documented compiled in the mid-seventh century— over the traditional Christian view based on many more, and much earlier, sources. He does, however, provide a rationale for this, and one that is becoming more and more popular. First, Fatoohi argues that the traditional biblical sources for Jesus' life are terribly unreliable, that they are filled with internal contradictions as well as historical inaccuracies. In fact, apart from those who take a "faith-driven approach" to the Bible, "scholars," he claims, "are unanimous that the Bible contains clear inaccuracies and mistakes."[8] This is indeed an interesting claim, given that there is a tremendous amount of scholarship, which Fatoohi conveniently ignores, that arrives at the opposite conclusion.[9] Nevertheless, his attack on the reliability of the

---

[7] There are numerous books available on Jesus in Islamic thought. Fatoohi's series of books on the subject—*Mystery of the Historical Jesus* (Birmingham: Luna Plena, 2007), *The Mystery of the Crucifixion* (Birmingham: Luna Plena, 2008), *The Mystery of the Messiah* (Birmingham: Luna Plena, 2009), and *Jesus: The Muslim Prophet* (Birmingham: Luna Plena, 2010)—are all representative of mainstream Islamic thought on Jesus. For a more progressive yet scholarly account see Neal Robinson, *Christ in Islam and Christianity* (Albany: SUNY Press, 1991).

[8] Fatoohi, *Mystery of the Historical Jesus*, 23.

[9] The literature on the continuity and historical reliability of the Bible is, to put it mildly, extensive. A good place to start, however, is with F. F. Bruce, *The New Testament Documents: Are They Reliable?* (Grand Rapids: Eerdmans, 1998), and Walter C. Kaiser, Jr., *The Old Testament Documents: Are they Reliable and Relevant?* (Downers Grove, IL: InterVarsity, 2001). To study the historical, archeological, and textual particularities and difficulties of the Bible, see the *Archeological Study*

Bible, and especially the Gospels, is polemically necessary. For if it can be shown that Jesus did not view himself as—or do anything to prove himself to be—divine, then there really is no good reason to confess his deity. The suggestion that such a doctrine was invented by the church therefore seems plausible if not probable. Moreover, in Fatoohi's mind, this would make the Qur'an a potentially more relevant and reliable source for considering the life (and nature) of Jesus.

Thus Fatoohi builds his argument by taking specific aim at the reliability of the Gospel records. His first argument draws upon the attack on the Gospel accounts made particularly popular by Walter Bauer's *Orthodoxy and Heresy in Earliest Christianity*. It runs like this: contemporary scholarship on the historical Jesus has demonstrated that the selection and adoption of Matthew, Mark, Luke, and John as the authoritative biographical sources on Jesus' life was completely arbitrary, for there are a host of other ancient (and, deemed by the church, non-canonical) Gospels that describe Jesus differently yet could very well contain accurate reports of him. Though there are more, Fatoohi cites—and uses—*The Infancy Gospel of James, The Gospel of the Birth of Mary, The Arabic Gospel of the Infancy, The Infancy Gospel of Thomas,* and *The Gospel of Pseudo-Matthew* to show that there are contradictions in the early biographical accounts of Jesus. To take the four canonical Gospels as the only reliable ones, he then concludes, is an arbitrary and certainly not a historically informed choice.

Fatoohi's second argument against the reliability of the Gospels is largely informed by contemporary biblical criticism. He is particularly fond of, and relies largely upon (as do a number of other Muslim apologists), the work of Bart Ehrman, especially his *Misquoting Jesus*. The argument here is, essentially, that amidst the thousands of manuscripts of the New Testament there are hundreds of thousands of textual variants. So even if the canonical books of the New Testament, especially the Gospels, are more reliable in

---

Bible (Grand Rapids: Zondervan, 2005) and *The Apologetics Study Bible* (Nashville: Holman, 2007).

comparison to the other ancient sources on Jesus, they still cannot be trusted. But whereas Ehrman himself admits that most of the variants "are completely insignificant, immaterial, of no real importance other than showing that scribes could not spell or keep focused any better than the rest of us," and only speculates that there must have been some purposeful altering of the text to suit a particular theological agenda, Fatoohi asserts as a matter of fact that "what we have today [in the canonical Gospels] is substantially edited and changed texts."[10] They may bear traces of real historical events and statements of Jesus; but, he contends, they have been corrupted with invented historical narratives, such as the crucifixion of Jesus, and various idiosyncratic theological alterations and additions, particularly with the identification of Jesus as God in the flesh. These certainly, Fatoohi confidently asserts, "were never part of the Injīl [Gospel] and were added by their respective authors and editors."[11]

This argument, which is ultimately derived from the quranic teaching that Jews and Christians tampered with and corrupted the once-reliable Bible (generally referred to as *tahrif*), has been a standard point in historic Muslim polemics against Christianity. Muslims apologists have even invented accounts of how the biblical text, which the Qur'an also endorses as revelatory (in the original autographs), was corrupted. An example of this is Fatoohi's treatment of John 14:16. He makes the rather startling assertion, though he admits there is "no direct evidence," that the original Gospel recorded Jesus promising the *periklytos*, or one who is "highly praised" (Ahmad in Arabic), and not the *parakletos*, or comforter (identified, by comparing with other biblical texts, as the Holy Spirit), found in extant copies of the Gospel of John.[12] Had the church allowed the

---

[10] Fatoohi, *Mystery of the Historical Jesus*, 26. The quotation from Ehrman's *Misquoting Jesus: The Story Behind Who Changed the Bible and Why* (San Francisco: Harper, 2007) is from pages 207–8.

[11] Fatoohi, *Mystery of the Historical Jesus*, 38.

[12] Fatoohi, *The Mystery of the Historical Jesus*, 375–77. Fatoohi borrows this argument from 'Abu 'L-Ahad Dawud, *Muhammad in the Bible* (Qatar: The Ministry of Awqaf and Islamic Affairs, 1994), 198–223.

Greek text to remain as it was originally rendered, it would be obvious that Jesus was not referring to the third person of the Holy Trinity, which is yet another theological invention of the church denounced in the Qur'an (see 4:171). Rather Jesus was referring to the coming of Ahmad, which is another name for Muhammad.[13]

MUSLIM POLEMICS, MODERN SCHOLARSHIP, AND POPULAR HISTORICAL REVISIONISTS

As tenuous and contrived as this and other similar arguments are, they are still worth the Christian apologist's attention. The chief reason for this is that what were once regarded as idiosyncratically Muslim arguments are now being refashioned as arguments that coincide with the latest historical scholarship. This is particularly the case with the Muslim assertion that Christians both invented and changed the New Testament to support the doctrine of the deity of Christ. "The Qur'an point out 14 centuries ago," Fatoohi claims, "what historians, archaeologists, and even Biblicists started to accept only 2 centuries ago."[14]

What he is referring to, and much of the scholarship he uses, was set in motion as far back as the eighteenth century when G. E. Lessing (1729–1781) published the private research of the German deist Hermann Samuel Reimarus (1694–1768). Since then, a number of scholars have embarked on what is normally termed the quest for the historical Jesus. The premise for such studies was, and in many ways remains, the conviction that the life, teachings, and deeds of Jesus had been mythologized by theologians and even by the original biographers of Jesus, such that it was the duty of the modern scholar and his critical historical methods to uncover and disclose the "real" Jesus. The results of this quest are perhaps best seen in the work of Rudolf Bultmann (1884–1976). He argued, in various ways, that the

---

[13] Qur'an 61:6: "Jesus, son of Mary, said, 'Children of Israel, I am sent to you by God, confirming the Torah that came before me and bringing good news of a messenger to follow me whose name will be Ahmad.' "

[14] Fatoohi, *Mystery of the Historical Jesus*, 37.

Gospels (and the rest of the New Testament) were not reliable descriptions of the Jesus of history. They were, instead, reliable descriptions of how the Early Church envisioned and ultimately divinized the historical man from Nazareth named Jesus.

The same argument continues to be made, only now its details have reached a popular audience. Members of the Jesus Seminar, for example, shortly after its establishment in 1985, began to take what was once a scholarly endeavor (or at least had scholarly pretensions) and packaged it for mass consumption.[15] Dan Brown, in his book-turned-movie, *The Da Vinci Code* (and other literature like it) reached an even wider audience. Embedding an historical claim in an otherwise fictional text, he has the British Royal Historian Sir Leigh Teabing educate an uninformed investigator, Sophie Neveu, that the earliest Christians viewed Jesus as no more than a human prophet. It was men at the Council of Nicaea in 325 that were guilty of inventing the theological doctrine of his deity.[16]

This is the claim of university-based scholars too. For example, Ehrman, who is held by many to be one of the world's leading authorities on the Bible, claims that had Nicaea not taken place or if some other view of Jesus predominated "there would have been no doctrine of Christ as both fully divine and human."[17] The same assumptions underpin Reza Aslan's popular *Zealot: The Life and Times of Jesus of Nazareth*. The claim that Jesus was a zealous political revolutionary who was only viewed as the divine son of God decades after his death by St. Paul and the later Christian tradition is a common assumption amongst historians who *a priori* rule out the

---

[15] See Michael J. Wilkins and J. P. Moreland, eds., *Jesus Under Fire: Modern Scholarship Reinvents the Historical Jesus* (Grand Rapids: Zondervan, 1995), 2. On the dubious nature of much of what passes for scientific historical research into the life and teachings of Jesus, see Eta Linnemann, *Historical Criticism of the Bible: Methodology or Ideology*, trans Robert Yarbrough (Grand Rapids: Kregel, 2001).

[16] Dan Brown, *The Da Vinci Code* (New York: Anchor Books, 2003), 253.

[17] Bart Ehrman, *Lost Christianities* (New York: Oxford University Press, 2003), 248.

possibility of an incarnation. While this is fairly standard fare in the realm of the so-called scholarly quest for the historical Jesus, its presence can in fact be traced back to a much earlier date in Muslim polemical literature. Al-Jabbār's early eleventh century *Critique of Christian Origins* makes the same claim as many contemporary western authors: that Christ's deity as a doctrine was invented at Nicaea and then arbitrarily imposed upon Christendom. The real religion of Jesus, and the theology of his initial followers, was much more akin to, if not equivalent to, Islamic monotheism.[18] Thus, the deity of Christ, writes Fatoohi, can certainly be regarded by any rational person (and not just Muslims) as a "Christian invention," for there is no good historical reason, nor has there ever been, to regard Jesus as divine.[19]

A RESPONSE TO MUSLIM POLEMICS

Obviously such a claim strikes at the very heart of Christianity. The divine nature of Christ is, as Jesus himself put it in Matthew 16:16–19, the rock upon which Christianity stands. This is the case in terms of its soteriology, for it was in the person and through the work of Christ that God reconciled the world unto himself (2 Corinthians 5:19); but it is also fundamental to the basic veracity of Christianity, for without a divine Christ the exclusive truth claims of Christianity ring hollow. Theological reasons notwithstanding, however, there is also a very practical reason that one be prepared to defend the orthodox (biblical) view of Jesus. It is, simply put, that Christians are not the only ones speaking of, claiming to represent, or answering questions about Jesus these days. Nor have we ever been. Islam, Hinduism, and other religions, as well as a cabal of atheists, have their own peculiar views of Jesus.[20] The difference now is that

---

[18] Al-Jabbār, *Critique of Christian Origins*, 5–7.

[19] Fatoohi, *Jesus the Muslim Prophet*, 31.

[20] See, for example, Gregory A. Barker and Stephen E. Gregg, eds, *Jesus beyond Christianity: The Classic Texts* (New York: Oxford University Press, 2010).

representatives of these worldviews are firmly embedded in what was once a country (or civilization) predominated by Christians, whereas in the past they were largely located on and contained within their native soil. Globalization, immigration, and the proliferation of information of all varieties and verities have changed public discourse on religion radically. Fatoohi's is just one example. So how does one respond to Fatoohi's argument that there is no historical evidence that Jesus was anything but a human, albeit a prophet of Islam. Is it true that there is no real objective evidence to suggest that Jesus was the son of God?

There are a number of ways to approach Fatoohi's argument as well as those of other Muslim apologists.[21] What follows is but one. It is, however, an argument that with appropriate alterations could be employed when facing any argument that at its base claims that there is no good reason to take Jesus as the divine son of God.

First, in the case of Fatoohi, it is necessary to start with a consideration of methodology or, rather, how one can or should approach the question of whether there is good reason to believe Jesus was divine. Despite his objective pretensions, Fatoohi's argument is anything but objective. In fact, while he can criticize Christianity for taking what he calls a "faith-driven approach" to the issue, he does exactly the same. He writes, "I need to make it clear that this book follows the Qur'anic approach. Any information in the canon, apocrypha, and history that is relevant to the subject of this book will first be presented and then explained from the Qur'an's point of view. Presuming that the Qur'an is the Word of God, this book seeks to show the consistency of the Qur'anic story of Jesus and its alignment with historical facts."[22]

---

[21] See, for example, Norman Anderson, *Islam in the Modern World: A Christian Perspective* (Leicester: Apollos, 1990), esp. 115–22; Norman L. Geisler and Abdul Saleeb, *Answering Islam: The Crescent in Light of the Cross* (Grand Rapids: Baker, 2002); Michael R. Licona, *Paul Meets Muhammad: A Christian-Muslim Debate on the Resurrection* (Grand Rapids: Baker, 2006); and the ever-helpful www.answering-islam.org.

[22] Fatoohi, *The Mystery of the Historical Jesus*, 41–42. On the circularity of Muslims apologetics, see John Warwick Montgomery, "How Muslims Do

There are all sorts of problems with this. First, there is the logical fallacy of assuming to be true what he is trying to prove (*petitio principii*). By his own admission, he assumes the historical truthfulness of the Qur'an from the beginning, and then interprets all evidence in light of what he already presumes to be true. Even more problematic, in purporting to explain or describe an historical person of the first century he gives evidential primacy to the allegedly historical reports contained in a text inscribed in, at the earliest, the mid-seventh century over and against material from the first century. There is no good reason for preferring the later Qur'an over earlier source material.[23] Fatoohi does not even bother trying to justify this preference based on historical grounds. This betrays the inherent epistemological weakness of his polemical apologetic. For Fatoohi, historical events, people, and ideas are understood and determined not by sources, artifacts, and other evidences emanating from or around the period under investigation, but instead by a book composed six hundred years later and, more importantly, by the ideology it contains. Like the Greek myth of Procrustes, who would force people into an iron bed whether they fit or not, Fatoohi puts his iron-clad faith commitments before and then imposes them upon his historical investigation. His ideology comes before and, then to confirm his

---

Apologetics," in *Faith Founded on Fact: Essays in Evidential Apologetics* (Edmonton: Canadian Institute for Law, Theology & Public Policy, 1978), 81–100.

[23] Moreover, the authenticity of the Qur'an as a text composed in the seventh century and "perfectly preserved" through the centuries is completely indefensible. Even early Muslims seem to have known this. For example, one tenth-century scholar and bibliophile from Baghdad, named al-Nadim, wrote, "I have seen a number of Qur'anic manuscripts. . . . No two of the Qur'anic copies were in agreement" (*The Fihrist of al-Nadim, a Tenth-Century Survey of Muslim Culture*, ed. Bayard Dodge [New York: Columbia, 1970], 57–58). See the first three chapters of Jane Dammen McAuliffe, ed., *The Cambridge Companion to the Qur'an* (New York: Cambridge University Press, 2006), 23–75 and Manfred S. Krop, ed., *Results of Contemporary Research on the Qur'an: The Question of a Historico-critical Text of the Qur'an* (Beirut: Ergon Verlag Würzburg, 2007).

bias, he interprets historical facts. This is manifest throughout his work, but where it is particularly obvious (and ludicrous) is in *The Mystery of the Crucifixion*, where he argues that Jesus was, as a matter of fact, not crucified; instead, he claims, early Christians invented the story to justify a theology they (Paul, especially) invented. Then, in repeating the story enough times and with enough conviction, they successfully convinced even their Jewish (e.g., Josephus) and Roman (e.g., Tacitus) adversaries, such that they mention in their own writings that Jesus died on a cross on a hill just outside of Jerusalem when Pontius Pilate was Prefect of Judea.

How, then, does he—and the overwhelming majority of Muslim tradition—justify what seems very much like a conspiracy theory? Not only do they *a priori* (before even examining evidence) assume the Qur'an is true in all it says (because it is, on an even more fundamental level, assumed to be the word of the creator), but apologists like Fatoohi operate with a coherence—as opposed to a correspondence—theory of truth. That is, our knowledge—true knowledge—of the extra-mental world (both present and historical) is not determined or verified to be true on the basis of its correspondence or linking up with the affairs of the world. Rather, according to the coherence view, what determines a belief or proposition about history is its coherence within an assumed network of beliefs. But this tells us nothing about what is in fact the case about Jesus. It is merely an assertion, one that is not only presumptuous but also erroneous.

Fatoohi's dismissal of the Gospels as reliable historical documents is also flawed. The Gospels—Matthew, Mark, Luke, and John—are in fact the primary documents from which any serious consideration of the historical Jesus must begin. That there are other ancient sources, most of which provide contradictory pictures of Jesus, is true. But just because they are ancient does not mean they are good sources. Scholarly—not sensational—criticism has demonstrated that all of the non-canonical gospels (the ones Fatoohi uses, as well as others) were written several generations after Jesus' death by authors who, therefore, had no direct or even indirect contact with Jesus.[24] The canonical Gospels, on the other hand, were written by eyewitnesses of Jesus' life (Matthew and John) or companions of the eyewitnesses (Mark and Luke). Fatoohi objects, of course, citing the fact that the author's names were not affixed to them until the late second century. He believes that the authorship of the four Gospels was made up to guarantee their acceptance over against emerging gnostic and other non-canonical gospel traditions. The canonical Gospels, he writes, "appear to have been quoted in the 1st half of the 2nd century, but always anonymously. They start to appear titled around 180 CE, but by then there were many gospels, not only the four."[25] Interestingly, here Fatoohi admits the earlier authorship of the Gospels of Matthew, Mark, Luke, and John, as opposed to the later authorship of the non-canonical gospels. Yet he engages in speculation as to why the names affixed to them appear so seemingly late: "[H]ad the author of any of these Gospels been a credible firsthand observer of the events or a disciple of Jesus he would have undoubtedly made this clear to distinguish his Gospel from competing writings and add credibility to it."[26] Matthew, Mark, Luke, and John were in fact credible biographers of Jesus (writing not modern but Hellenistic biographies).[27] They did not need to attach their names to the Gospels they wrote, for what mattered to them was not the authority of the author but the events they recorded and passed on to persuade their readers that Jesus was the Christ, the son of the living God. The events recorded in the Gospel accounts were written with the assumption that the reader could, if he or she desired, verify their

---

[24] For detailed accounts, see, among others, Lee Strobel, *The Case for the Real Jesus* (Grand Rapids: Zondervan, 2007), 23–63; Darrell L. Bock, *The Missing Gospels* (Nashville: Nelson, 2006); Craig Evans, *Fabricating Jesus: How Modern Scholars Distort the Gospel* (Downers Grove, IL: InterVarsity, 2006).

[25] Fatoohi, *Mystery of the Historical Jesus*, 28.

[26] Fatoohi, *Mystery of the Historical Jesus*, 28.

[27] Richard Burridge, *What Are the Gospels? A Comparison with Greco-Roman Biography* (Grand Rapids: Eerdmans, 2004).

facticity.[28] Further, the question of the authorship of the Gospels is not an unsettled issue. Both Irenaeus (c. 130–202) and the even earlier Papias (c. 70–155) identify the authors of the Gospels as those who were either eyewitness of Jesus' life or their close companions. In the words of Irenaeus, which also echo those of his predecessor,

> Matthew published his Gospel . . . when Peter and Paul were preaching the gospel in Rome and founding the church there [c. 60s]. After their departure [i.e. death], Mark, the disciple and interpreter of Peter, himself handed down to us in writingthe substance of Peter's preaching. Luke, the follower of Paul, set down in a book the gospel preached by his teacher. Then John, the disciple of the lord . . . himself produced his Gospel, while he was living at Ephesus in Asia.[29]

The historian, alongside and even before the faith-driven Christian, can conclude—for there is no evidence to the contrary, nor is their reason to suspect some sort of theological conspiracy theory—that Matthew, Mark, Luke, and John are primary documents attesting to the life of Jesus.

The question that soon follows, though, is: are they reliable? That is, has the testimony and research of Matthew, Mark, Luke, and John been preserved well-enough through the centuries that we can trust it? The answer is a resolute yes.[30] There are, to be sure, thousands of copyist errors found among the thousands of manuscript copies of the New Testament. This is to be expected from literature emerging in eras long before word processors with spell-checkers and other modern conveniences that authors enjoy. Moreover, scholars—Christian and non-Christian—have studied these since the early eighteenth century, when the first critical edition of the New

---

[28] This is evident outside the Gospels as well, as, e.g., in 1 Corinthians 15:6, where Paul refers to more than 500 witnesses of the resurrection, most of whom remain alive.

[29] Irenaeus, *Adversus haereses,* III.1.

[30] See chapter 2 of this volume.

Testament was published, and have repeatedly found that none of the errors is of great significance, and certainly none alters the theology of the text. A full ninety-nine percent of them consist of spelling variations, changes in word order, the substitution of words for synonyms (e.g., replacing a pronoun with its proper nominal referent), and other similarly insignificant matters.[31] Thus, sober-minded scholars specializing in the transmission of the New Testament text remain confident that *"there are no significant variants from any manuscript of any age"* suggesting the text is untrustworthy.[32] So there is no evidentially supportable reason to suggest the description of Jesus as divine was added into the text of the Gospels (and the rest of the New Testament) by some ecclesiastical faction with a high christology. Nor is there reason to suggest that words were put into Jesus' mouth when he responded in the affirmative to the question of whether he was divine (e.g., Mark 14:62). After all, it was on the charge of blasphemy for which he was arrested.

Nevertheless, it is of course one thing to claim deity and quite another to prove it. Such proof or vindication of all Jesus' claims is his resurrection. This, too, Fatoohi obviously denies. He claims, as Muslims traditionally have, that Jesus never even died. This is taught explicitly in Qur'an 4:157–158, which states that Jesus was neither killed nor crucified, but that it only appeared so to the disciples; instead, Jesus simply ascended into heaven. Going beyond the Qur'an, the Islamic exegetical tradition explains that what happened was that in the midst of Jesus' last supper with his disciples he managed quietly to slip away, while someone else (most say Judas)

---

[31] The two big issues concerning the transmission of the gospels are the ending of the gospel of Mark (16:9–20) and the story of the woman caught in adultery in John 7:53–8:11. The earliest manuscripts do not contain these passages. Why they are missing from them but contained in later manuscripts still baffles scholars.

[32] J. Ed Komoszewski, M. James Sawyer, and Daniel B. Wallace, *Reinventing Jesus: How Contemporary Skeptics Miss the Real Jesus and Mislead Popular Culture* (Grand Rapids: Kregel, 2006), 117. (Emphasis in the original.)

was made to appear like him and was then crucified in his place.[33] This is a common polemic in Muslim apologetics, for as one of its vociferous exponents put it in a widely-distributed pamphlet, "If Jesus did NOT die, and he was NOT resurrected from the dead, there can be NO salvation in Christianity! . . . In a nutshell, No Crucifixion!—No Christianity!"[34]

If this argument were true it would indeed be destructive to Christianity. The problem is, simply, that it is absurd. That Jesus died on a cross is, even the most ardent skeptics acknowledge, "as sure as anything historical ever can be."[35] This is obviously clear not only from the early and reliable testimony of the New Testament, but is also corroborated by the independent testimony of other ancient, even hostile, authors such as Josephus, Tacitus, Mara bar-Serapion, and the authors of the Talmud.[36] The resurrection, likewise, is a demonstrable historical event. The eyewitness testimony itself is enough to establish it as a matter of fact (as Craig Parton argues in chapter 3 of this volume). It was Jesus' resurrection from the dead that decisively settled for men like Thomas and the earliest Christians the troubles they had with acknowledging the divine nature of Jesus; "All their doubts," wrote Clement of Rome at the end of the first century, "had been set at rest by the resurrection."[37] It is hardly a stretch to say that there is no way the Christian church would have ever come into existence and rose to prominence had Jesus not risen from the dead, for had the things the church said about Jesus (and especially about his resurrection) not transpired, it could have been easily falsified in

---

[33] On historical Muslim thought and the crucifixion, see Todd Lawson, *The Crucifixion and the Qur'an: A Study in the History of Muslim Though* (Oxford: Oneworld Publications, 2009).

[34] Ahmed Deedat, "Crucifixion or Cruci-Fiction? in *The Choice: Islam and Christianity*, vol. 2 (New Delhi: Adam Publishers, 2004), 147.

[35] John Dominic Crossan, *Jesus: A Revolutionary Biography* (San Francisco: HarperCollins, 1991), 145.

[36] See the interview with Michael Licona in Strobel's *The Case for the Real Jesus*, 113–14.

[37] 1 Clement 42:3.

the very city in which the church was born—Jerusalem. All that had to be done was for someone to produce the body of Jesus; and Christianity's Jewish and Roman enemies alike had every means, motive, and opportunity to do so. They did not and could not, though, for the tomb was empty. And it was the empty tomb that produced in early Christians, as even their Roman persecutor Pliny the Younger (c. 61–112) observed, "the habit of meeting on a certain fixed day before sunrise and reciting an antiphonal hymn to [him] as God."[38]

CONCLUSION

The evidence of the life of Jesus himself, and from the records of Jesus' life, all point to the fact that God was in Christ Jesus. The Muslim's commitment to the Qur'an, and corresponding rejection of the biblical record, are perhaps the largest hurdle any Christian facing the claims of Islam will encounter. The Muslim is under the impression that the Christian holds to the reliability of the Gospels merely as a matter of faith. This is not requisite though. That the Gospels are reliable primary-source material for the life and teachings of Jesus, and that the non-canonical gospels are not, is a matter of basic historiography. What is in no way a conclusion of reason based on the consideration of the evidence is Fatoohi's elevation of the Qur'an as the lens through which history is viewed. This is completely arbitrary—an act of faith, as Fatoohi admits, and in no way the result of objective historiographical reasoning. To then suppose some concerted process of altering the text of the Gospels to fit a particular theological agenda proves to be mere speculation at best and conspiracy theorizing at worst. But it is perhaps understandable. After all, how else can the Muslim explain the competing versions of Jesus in the Bible and the Qur'an? The Gospels clearly regard Jesus as divine whereas the Qur'an regards him as only a man. But it is not just Jesus' claims about himself in the Gospels and the affirmations of the New Testament writers that contradict the Qur'an; it is the deeds he performed that do so as well. Jesus'

---

[38] Pliny, *Epistles*, 10:96.

crucifixion and resurrection from the dead, both of which are confirmed by extra-biblical sources, not only contradict the Qur'an's testimony on the events of Jesus' last days on earth. They also contradict its claim that he was merely a man, for the resurrection of Jesus clearly points to his divine nature. Any person—Muslim or non-Muslim—considering just who Jesus was (and is) must consider these facts, and the conclusions they draw must conform to the facts. Believing anything else is tantamount to believing a myth—the myth of a Muslim prophet named Jesus in this case—even if it is dressed up with superficial historical reasoning and backed by a purportedly sacred text.

FOR FURTHER READING

Anderson, Norman. *Islam in the Modern World: A Christian Perspective.* Leicester: Apollos, 1990.

Bowman, Robert M. and J. Ed Komoszewski. *Putting Jesus in His Place: The Case for the Deity of Christ.* Grand Rapids: Kregel, 2007.

Evans, Craig A. *Fabricating Jesus: How Modern Scholars Distort the Gospels.* Downers Grove, IL: InterVarsity, 2006.

Geisler, Norman L. and Abdul Saleeb. *Answering Islam: The Crescent in Light of the Cross.* Grand Rapids: Baker, 2002.

Komoszewski, J. Ed, M. James Sawyer, and Daniel B. Wallace. *Reinventing Jesus: How Contemporary Skeptics Miss the Real Jesus and Mislead Popular Culture.* Grand Rapids: Kregel, 2006.

Licona, Michael R. *Paul Meets Muhammad: A Christian-Muslim Debate on the Resurrection.* Grand Rapids: Baker, 2006.

Montgomery, John Warwick. *History, Law and Christianity.* Edmonton: Canadian Institute for Law, Theology, and Public Policy Inc., 2002.

Skarsaune, Oskar. *Incarnation: Myth or Fact?* Translated by Trygve R. Skarsten. St. Louis: Concordia, 1991.

Strobel, Lee. *The Case for the Real Jesus.* Grand Rapids: Zondervan, 2007.

Swinburne, Richard. *Was Jesus God?* New York: Oxford University Press, 2010.

_____. *The Resurrection of God Incarnate.* New York: Oxford University Press, 2003.

Wilkins, Michael J. and J. P. Moreland. *Jesus Under Fire: Modern Scholarship Reinvents the Historical Jesus.* Grand Rapids: Zondervan, 1995.

5

THE SCANDAL
OF CHRISTIAN PARTICULARITY

John Bombaro

THE FAIRNESS DOCTRINE
AND THE PROBLEM OF RESTRICTIVISM

The issue of Christian particularity, the doctrine that salvation is found in Christ alone with the consequence that some are not saved but damned, is perhaps (along with the doctrine of original sin) the most hotly contested tenet of the faith. And for good reason: the very notion of God actually damning those who reject or, worse still, are not afforded the opportunity to hear and respond to the good news of God's love is dismissed out of hand as cruel and irrational. To espouse belief in a God who damns those who are without witness to his saving efforts makes a monster out of the Almighty. It just isn't fair, and if it isn't fair (as the thinking goes), then it isn't true. This is why the idea of salvation by Christ alone through faith alone bears the pejorative moniker, "the scandal of particularity."

The "scandal" of particularity is precisely this: If the Christian faith is objectively true and "there is no other name under heaven given among men by which we much be saved" (Acts 4:12) than that of Jesus Christ of Nazareth, then innumerable people who have been either misinformed or uninformed about Jesus the Savior will be condemned since "there is salvation in no one else." Not to be saved through Christ alone is to be left alone in judgment. Christian particularity is a problem because it espouses a *particular* revelation (the Bible), entrusted to a *particular* people (Jews then Christians), regarding a *particular* event of salvation (by Jesus of Nazareth). "Particular" means specific and specific means exclusive. And exclusive, in today's intellectual and sentimental climate, is intolerably unfair, indeed, scandalous, especially when talking about religion.

To be sure, the problem of Christian particularism is tethered to the issue of theodicy, and critics of orthodox Christianity are quick to exploit the connection between the two. "How can a good and loving God," they ask, "who is sovereign and providential and therefore ultimately responsible for the dissemination and application of the Gospel, be the cause of such unjust and unreasonable condemnation?"

How can people be judged on the basis of something they don't know? What kind of "good news" tells a story with such a bad ending for the tribes of Papua New Guinea and the bush people of Africa who have never even heard the story in the first place? It just isn't fair. If God is good and loving, then he must adjudicate according to the unfairness of the situation and pardon anyone who has not been exposed to the Gospel. Christian particularism as exclusivism must, therefore, be rejected on account of its scandalous restrictivism. If this is the only way, then the answer is no way. Or so the thinking goes in an age of cherished pluralism.

DAWKINS AND THE FAIRNESS DOCTRINE

Objections to Christian particularism arise from a worldview that emerges from the metanarrative—the overarching account or all-encompassing story that gives semblance and meaning to the historical record, or *the* story that governs all other stories—of Scripture being rejected in part or entirely. Contemporary objections both within Christianity and outside are therefore conditioned by the way people understand the story of the world, with corresponding ideas about what is and is not fair, as well as related views pertaining to the nature of humankind (e.g., whether humankind is basically good or not). Consideration will be given to each of these concerns within the scope of a conversation about what is being dubbed here *the fairness doctrine*. The idea of fairness plays no small role in the current debate regarding Christian particularism. The fairness doctrine permits that the "good news of God" can be embraced (or at least tolerated), so long as it does not come with corresponding bad news from God, or anyone else for that matter.

Oxford University professor and renowned atheist Richard Dawkins typifies this, pushing the solution to the problem of particularity to the (political) extreme. For Dawkins, Christianity is the invention of warped religious fanatics, further perverting the already perverted God-concept of Judaism. He sees Christianity as *just* the religious things people do and believe in the tradition "Christian." Again, there is nothing special about Christianity other than it is the world's most populous religion, which is a problem because Christianity retards human progress with cruel and irrational teachings, alienating the truthful Darwinian worldview of materialism. In *The God Delusion*, he writes:

> New Testament theology adds a new injustice [to the Old Testament depiction of God], topped off by a new sadomasochism whose viciousness even the Old Testament barely exceeds. . . . God incarnated himself as a man, Jesus, in order that he should be tortured and executed in *atonement* for the hereditary sin of Adam. Ever since Paul expounded this repellant doctrine, Jesus has been worshipped as the *redeemer* of all our sins. . . . I have described atonement, the central doctrine of Christianity, as vicious, sadomasochistic and repellant. We should also dismiss it as barking mad, but for its ubiquitous familiarity which has dulled our objectivity. If God wanted to forgive our sins, why not just forgive them, without having himself tortured and executed in payment[?][1]

Dawkins identifies three inherently scandalous things about Christianity: the sinfulness of humanity, the righteousness of God's judgment, and the cross of Christ as the means of redemption whereby some but not all are saved. What may seem to be blasphemous language isn't for Dawkins. His worldview is the product of post-Kantian Darwinism in which the material world is the *only* reality. His commitment to the fairness doctrine compels him to say, as it were, "Since these preposterous teachings of the Bible are all the product of human imagination, and since in our enlightened scientific age such teachings are distasteful, then it behooves Christianity either to amend its fundamental teachings about sin, righteousness, and judgment, or disband; for such teachings in our materialist world border criminality." So while for some (such as Universalists), the God of Judeo-Christianity must be fair to all; for atheists like Dawkins, since there is no God and religion is make-

---

[1] Richard Dawkins, *The God Delusion* (Houghton Mifflin: New York, 2006), 251, 252, 253.

believe anyway, Christianity is unfair and hateful to most, even to Jesus himself and, therefore, is rightly ridiculed and condemned and should be outlawed from public discourse. For him, it's the only fair thing to do.

Dawkins' appraisement of Christianity comports with the fairness doctrine's boundaries for the socially acceptable. At the heart of his increasingly prevalent worldview is the intellectual commitment to the Kantian Divide, the unscalable wall between the phenomenal and noumenal, the real and the unreal, the natural and the "supernatural." (There is no empirical evidence or way to verify noumenal holdings; it is purely an academic designation for speculative metaphysical concepts.) Knowledge is limited only to that sphere of existence to which we have access: the phenomenological realm. Therefore, it is unfair to ask those who live in the objectively real to be subject to superstitious ignoramuses who propose life according to their divisive, subjective unrealities.

THE HISTORICAL-FACTUAL BASIS
OF CHRISTIAN FAITH AND DOCTRINE

But the storyline of Scripture is not about subjectivism, not about an internal religion, not about spirituality, not about the religious things Jews and Christians do, not about ethics. Rather, the burden of the Judeo-Christian Scriptures is about news, reports of events, phenomena that occurred in real human history. Michael Horton states it this way:

> The central message of Christianity is not a worldview, a way of life, or a program for personal or societal change; it is a gospel. From the Greek word for "good news," typically used in the context of announcing a military victory, the *gospel* is the report of an appointed messenger who arrives from the battlefield. That is why the New Testament refers to the offices of apostle (official representative), preacher, and evangelist, describing ministers as heralds, ambassadors, and witnesses. Their job is to get the story right and report it,

ensuring that the message is delivered by word (preaching) and deed (sacrament). And the result is a church, an embassy of the triune God in the midst of this passing evil age, with the whole people of God giving witness to God's mighty acts of redemption.

It is not incidental, then, that this story of redemption is called *Good News*. If it were merely information or a program for self-improvement, it would be called something else, like *good advice* or *a good idea* or *good enlightenment*. But it's Good News because it is an announcement of something that someone else has already achieved for us.[2]

Truly newsworthy items happen; they are events that occur outside of us. Broadcasting the feelings or impressions inside of us is called *opinion*. Thus, news is a particular kind of communication. Eyewitness news concerns events, phenomenological occurrences in real human history. The news pertains to the objective not the subjective. Significantly, the accounts of the Bible are given to us not in terms of "we believe *in*" but "we testify *that*." And what follows are things melded to public happenings, things bound up with the character and reputation of the reporters. Indeed, even when there is a subjective component, say, a prophetic word from the Lord to a herald like Isaiah, the verity of the message is always tethered to present or future historical situations or events and, therefore, open to public investigation and scrutiny.

This is what Christianity proclaims: News. And the news, put into Kantian terms, is good: *the noumenal became phenomenal*. There was a phenomenological occurrence by the noumenal and it was Jesus Christ. Though we might not be able to move from the phenomenal realm to the noumenal, yet with the incarnation the eternal touches time, supernatural becomes natural, the metaphysical dons physicality, the unseen is seen, grace invades nature. The apostle in 1 John 1:1–3 uses the most graphic phenomenological terms possible

---

[2] Michael Horton, *Christless Christianity: The Alternative Gospel of the American Church* (Grand Rapids: Baker, 2008), 105.

to articulate the tangible, spatiotemporal reality what took place with the incarnation (emphasis added):

> That which was from the beginning, which we have *heard*, which we have *seen with our eyes*, which we *looked upon* and have *touched with our hands*, concerning the word of life— the life was *made manifest*, and *we have seen it*, and testify to it and proclaim to you the eternal life, which was with the Father and was *made manifest to us*—that which *we have seen and heard* we proclaim also to you, so that you too may have fellowship with us; and indeed our fellowship is with the Father and with his Son Jesus Christ.

The entire Bible stands and falls with the phenomenological *manifestation* of God in human reality, which is why stories of the Bible are bound to verifiable historical locations, times, peoples, and events: theological veracity is necessarily tethered to the historical method. Luke opens his investigative report of the Good News with these words: "In the days of Herod, king of Judea" (1:5) and continues in chapter two, noting, "In those days a decree went out from Caesar Augustus that all the world should be registered. This was the first registration when Quirinius was governor of Syria" (2:1–2). So far from happening "in a galaxy far, far away," the news of the Bible is that it happened "over there, right then, among them." This is why the disciplines of biblical historiography, biblical anthropology, and biblical archeology are not pseudo-sciences. They deal with the real. They are concerned with the truth. Those who would like to dismiss Christianity as utterly subjective or merely ethical or perhaps purely metaphysical, like Dawkins, only do so by way of an inconsistent commitment to the methodological principles of historical investigation.[3] Christianity has its foundation in

---

[3] John Warwick Montgomery explains the importance of this point: "the documentary attestation for these [biblical events] is so strong that a denial of their reliability carries with it total skepticism toward the history and literature of the classical world." *History and Christianity: A Vigorous, Convincing Presentation of the Evidence for a Historical Jesus* (Minneapolis: Bethany House Publishers, 1964), 43. Cf. Jaroslav Pelikan,

phenomenological reality that fortifies its teaching the truth about sin, salvation and the rule of God, not just for Christians but for all people.

BIBLICAL PARTICULARISM

Critical in the Christian response to ideological fairness is the objectivity of the Bible's story. This is where the Christian begins the apologetic task—with something that *happened* not with feelings or opinions. The historical events, locations, and persons that facilitate biblical episodes of divine self-disclosure are not accidental or incidental. They are culturally meaning-laden and therefore set the parameters of understanding for who God is, how God is, what God does, and why God does it. God does not leave his words, actions, and reputation open to interpretation. He seals them in the objectivity of historical events, altering talk about God from the subjective to the objective, from feelings back to facts, where Christianity it at home.

What is more, the events of biblical history are not a bunch of random happenings, nor are they universal (occurring to all people equally). If that were the case, it would be difficult, if not impossible, to distinguish any meaningful action or characteristic of God. Instead, the events are particularized, consciously bound to one another as an organic whole and articulated within the pages of the Bible as of a piece comprising a single grand narrative. Presenting themselves for the most part in a linear fashion, they take up one another because each episode entails an eschatological component—each is forward looking, emblematic (typological), goal-oriented (telic). Biblical events are fixed entities of history whose penultimate meaning moves through history, recapitulating preceding epochs, but with added disclosures and clarifications, to an ultimate event with conclusive significance. Consequently, they never stand in isolation as abstractions but occur in public relation to one another, even among other people groups, who may corroborate their authenticity, like the

---

The Vindication of Tradition (New Haven: Yale University Press, 1984), 43–61.

people of Jericho who (like international correspondents) testified to Israel's miraculous exodus from Egypt, though Yahweh was not their God (Joshua 2:8–11). Making the case for Christianity means conversing about reality: Christians are to present the Bible's total story being entrenched in the real, just as St Paul said: "I am speaking true and rational words . . . for this has not been done in a corner" (Acts 26:25–26).

The events in Scripture that invite investigation are further objectified when identified with a particular people group—the Hebrews. The Hebrews are important to making the case because of their reputation as a candid, self-critical, and truthful people. In ancient Semitic culture a person was as their word.[4] If you lied, you were a liar, the son of a liar, the grandson of a liar; your children were liars. Your word was your reputation and your reputation had implications for the collective lives of your family members for generations since there was no such thing as an individual in the modern sense.[5] It is important that *this* kind of people, reliable and brutally honest, be the field correspondents reporting the news of God's redemptive words and actions.

Not only are the events and people specified, but the message and effect of the historical events are specified. Unlike a news channel claiming simply to report, while "you decide," biblical witnesses report the event and herald or proclaim its meaning and significance, too. For example, the writers of the New Testament not only say, "We saw Jesus alive after his public execution and so did hundreds of others," but "this is what that event means within this ongoing story of God's action, presence and purposes in the world" (see, e.g., 1 Corinthians 15). It is this kind of historical, cultural, anthropological, and documentary objectivity about things done in public among trustworthy people that invites all to consider the preponderance of evidence regarding a very specific message: the Gospel of the Lord Jesus.

---

[4] See Bruce J. Malina, *The New Testament World: Insights from Cultural Anthropology* (Louisville: Westminster, 1993 revised edition), *passim*.

[5] Malina, *The New Testament World*, 67.

A *particular* people, during *particular* times, in *particular* locations, enduring and witnessing *particular* events have yielded a *particular* message (in keeping with the storyline that preceded it), so that who this God is and what he is doing is clear and simple. Christian particularism as exclusivism is all about keeping the contents of Christianity in the sphere of the real, where we come to know the truth. The promise-making God proves himself the promise-keeping God in the recovery of his global kingdom by a first century Jew about whom not only his contemporaries Matthew, Mark, Luke, John, Paul, and Peter write, but also non-Christians like Josephus and even enemies of the faith, too, like Tacitus, Pliny, and Suetonius. Public testimony about Jesus is in perfect keeping with the preceding background story of God's solution for the world's rebellion that focused on Israel, itself a public entity. Understood within the light of the total story of the Bible, the scandal of particularity as exclusivity undergoes clarification as *God's personal presence and specified performance in the pursuit of the lost.* God was not leaving his actions and their meaning to chance, relativism, or subjectivity. The Lord's pointed action in a particular person was not for precluding people groups but keeping the story consistent so that all might know and share in the truth, both Jew and Gentile (Ephesians 3:1–11).

Thus, the response to those who espouse the fairness doctrine is set within the wider setting of the biblical story, since Scripture bears witness to the truth that God's particularized events and means reveal *salvific specificity*, not bigoted exclusivity. It turns out that the specified means of grace committed to a specified people (Christians) make finding God *easier* but also make who he is and what he is doing more readily identifiable and understandable.

KINGDOM AS KEY

God gives specifics about his specificity in the Bible for our assurance that it is in fact the true God and not the figment of imaginations. To ascertain this specificity, it is important for readers of the Bible to recognize that *biblical interpretation begins within the Bible itself* in the same way that a roadmap interprets itself through its in-built "legend" or "key." There are established ruling principles of biblical interpretation that recognize the Bible's self-presenting, self-interpreting "legend" or "key," lending itself to a properly contextualized reading horizon.

That contextualized reading yields an already theologically interpreted text *as the history of the divine work of redemption*, thoroughly bonded to human history. Fundamental to this theological interpretation is the principle metaphor through which the entire story in all of its parts is articulated, namely the metaphor of "kingdom."

Recognizing that the metaphor of "kingdom" is the governing paradigm for conceiving and interpreting Scripture's metanarrative affects one's overall engagement with the text and immediately bears on Christian particularism. The concept of kingdom is not just present in specific words (e.g., "kingdom," "dominion," "Lord," etc.) but also in symbols and symbolic acts within the Bible. It fundamentally governs the reading horizon of the Bible by limiting the scope of interpretation due to the fact that the meanings of the Bible had their original context in a prior historical understanding of reality as hierarchical, authoritative, and regal. It is, simply, the lens through which the Bible is to be read. It is critical that this understanding be communicated to those who argue for religious relativism, since the Christian does not bear witness to *my* Lord, subjectively, but *the* Lord, objectively. The metaphor of kingdom will clarify some issues related to particularism as exclusivism because its dominant place in Scripture facilitates the way the world is to be viewed, not just in biblical times but all times. The task of the metaphor brings our worldviews, whatever they may be, into conformity with God's arrangement of the world.

Genesis 1 immediately institutes the kingdom motif. The image the creation account sets before the reader is one where the great King, whose priority is underscored by the fact that he establishes all subsequent relationships, issues forth his royal decree ("Let there be light") to which the only response can be, "And there was light" (1:3). Heaven will be his throne and the earth his footstool (Isaiah 66:1). The King establishes his earthly kingdom and creates his image-bearer, the one who stands in the King's stead—man. The image-bearer is the King's vice-regent, given "dominion" over the earthly kingdom and endowed with the glory-presence of the King's Spirit. The terms of this arrangement are understood within the context of a solemn covenant. The King offers a land-grant—the entire earthly kingdom—plus an even greater inheritance (sharing in the King's very life) but, commensurate with these privileges, he requires faultless service, imaging-forth his character and nature to the glory of his name. The covenant has great promises but also threats: lording in the Lord's stead contrary to his rule is to claim independent lordship and will be adjudicated as an act of treason tantamount to saying, "I will not have this King reign over us. I shall reign instead." So, too, siding with the King's enemy will be judged an act of high treason. The penalty for treason, of course, is death: "dying you shall surely die" (Genesis 2:17).

The image-bearer is therefore entrusted with the King's earthly rule, his name, and thus the security of his kingdom. As it is with the viceroy, so it may be assumed to be with the King. The King is as his Word, so, too, man shall be as the Word of God.

Significantly, the great King intimates that there is an enemy when he commands the man to "keep" or, better, "protect" the earthly kingdom (Genesis 2:15). And so there is. An enemy angles to usurp the lordship of the King by making a traitor or co-conspirator of the viceroy. The plot avails and the kingdom is usurped from the care of the image-bearer. The covenanted servant turns on the King. And now the earthly kingdom has a new lord and the viceroy has willfully fallen captive to the dominion of the King's enemy. Divested of the King's Spirit-presence, the scene of Genesis 3 is the record of mankind's fall from grace and high treason.

The events that follow all pertain to the rightful King's pursuit of his earthly kingdom and its citizenry. However, those who own the fairness doctrine will not be able to move beyond Genesis 3 without raising objections to human sin and the nature of divine judgment.

One frequented caricature is that the God of the Bible, especially as depicted in the Old Testament, is a violent, hot-tempered despot, wielding shockingly disproportionate punishments for the slightest peccadillo. Again, Richard Dawkins is typical. He wonders, "Why should a divine being, with creation and eternity on his mind, care a fig for petty human malefactions? We humans give ourselves such airs, even aggrandizing our poky little 'sins' to the level of cosmic significance."[6] First, Dawkins brings into question the nature of sin, whether sins are a serious matter, in his commentary on "the Old Testament myth of Adam and Eve":

> Their sin—eating the fruit of a forbidden tree—seems mild enough to merit a mere reprimand. But the symbolic nature of the fruit (knowledge of good and evil, which in practice turned out to be knowledge that they were naked) was enough to turn their scrumping escapade into the mother and father of all sins. They and all their descendants were banished forever from the Garden of Eden, deprived of the gift of eternal life, and condemnation to generations of painful labour, in the field and in childbirth respectively.[7]

Having concluded that sins are really nothing more than morally relative personal mistakes or violations of accepted social or legislated standards, he criticizes the Judeo-Christian God's "monumental rage" and "juridical brimstone" for sentencing his image-bearers to death. Dawkins does not acknowledge the governing metaphor of kingdom; instead the God of the Old Testament is for him "arguably the most unpleasant character in all fiction: jealous and proud of it; a petty, unjust, unforgiving control-freak; a vindictive, bloodthirsty ethnic cleanser; a misogynistic, homophobic, racist, infanticidal, genocidal, filicidal, pestilential, megalomaniacal, sadomasochistic, capriciously malevolent bully."[8] This is the scandal of Christian particularism as exclusivism: if a person is not saved by this God through faith in his specific and exclusive provision, Jesus the Christ, then they will be unfairly, unjustly, and unreasonably

---

[6] Dawkins, *The God Delusion*, 238.

[7] Dawkins, *The God Delusion*, 251.

[8] Dawkins, *The God Delusion*, 31.

condemned and punished. "What makes my jaw drop is that people today should base their lives on such an appalling role model as Yahweh—and, even worse, that they should bossily try to force the same evil monster (whether fact or fiction) on the rest of us."[9]

Dawkins would have a point if "our pokey little 'sins' " were just that—no big deal. Who is anyone wearing a clerical or cassock to say someone is a criminal deserving of death? I fudged my taxes a bit, yes; but a criminal deserving capital punishment? That's overkill.

Having addressed Dawkins' dismissal of the Bible's record of redemptive history as subjective "fiction," an honest reading of Scripture requires that the issue of sin and judgment be understood under the auspices of the kingdom metaphor, not the fairness doctrine. The punishment for high treason is death because high treason is the violation of allegiance toward one's sovereign, especially the betrayal of one's sovereign by cooperating in the usurping of the sovereign's rule or by consciously and purposely acting to aid and abet the sovereign's enemies. In other words, it is the willful act of betrayal that has as its purpose transferring the power of the kingdom to the sovereign's enemies. Such insidious treachery, the law says, warrants death just as it does in the United States, Israel, Brazil, nearly all countries of the Middle East, Sub-Continent, Africa, and most of Western Europe (at least until 1989 and later).

Given that the God of the Bible is the world's one and only true Lord to whom we owe allegiance, honor, respect, and duty, if sin is nothing other than willful rebellion and the conscripting or engendering of others against the Sovereign's right and will to rule, then what does the King's well-published decree say the wages of sin is? Death (Romans 6:23). Why is the wages of sin death? Because it *is* high treason against the Sovereign, with far-reaching ramifications for families, subsequent generations, and entire communities. God's governing in Scripture and even the way we govern ourselves testify that high treason is so destructive and dangerous to others, that

---

[9] Dawkins, *The God Delusion*, 248.

without a proportionate penalty, chaos and death would prevail. Judging high treason preserves the rule of law established by the Lord of the law.

Both Scripture and even a cursory examination of our lives evidence our high treason. The apostle Paul states it this way: "There is none righteous, no, not one: There is none that understands, there are none that seek after God. They are all gone out of the way, they are together become unprofitable; there is none that does good; no, not one" (3:11–12). In the view of Scripture, all have sinned and stand guilty of treason before the King, habitual offenders robbing God of his glory, honor, and praise, stealing it for ourselves or giving it to another master, saying, "I will not have him lord over me." This is a statement of self-sovereignty and therefore self-enthronement. Such repudiation of the kingship of God, whether with or without malice, garners the judgment of the King because it dangerously jeopardizes the wise rule of the King and therefore the rule of law. And so all the world stands guilty before the holy King's righteous law (for he is holy), and he pledges his word in covenant that he will uphold the terms that obligate and now condemn all humanity.

When sin is understood as high treason, then spinning it as merely missing the mark or a personal peccadillo utterly trivializes the seriousness of the crime. If the mark is exactitude in regal representation—as Jesus put it: "You therefore must be perfect, as your heavenly Father is perfect" (Matthew 5:48)—or, put differently, "holiness," then any infraction must be adjudicated as treason, even high treason.

Christians can facilitate profitable discussion by minimizing the caricaturing of sin and divine judgment, setting it in its historical and biblical (and even contemporary cultural) setting. When the truth about treason has been established, then the truth about pardon can be proclaimed. Humanity has a specific problem, not just sins—the treasonous things we think, say, and do—but a treasonous disposition, a nature given to rebellion. No one is exempt. In this humanity is unified. It is this nature and the fruit of our nature that leaves us condemned for treason before the great King.

The fairness doctrine does away with sin and in doing so does away with personal guilt for treasonous crimes committed against the Sovereign. And where there is no guilt, there can be no judgment. With no judgment, there is no need for a Savior. But take our natural propensity and disposition toward treason and therefore guilt seriously, that is, within the context of kingdom, then the world needs a Savior.

Biblical salvation is principally salvation from the King's judgment. All fall under that judgment because all come under the umbrella of his covenants and lordship, whether acknowledged or not. Such is the onus of the first commandment and of the prophets (Exodus 20:3–5; cf. Isaiah 43:3; 45:6, 18). And the only one with authority to pardon is, of course, the King himself. At this point Richard Dawkins' query would seem to have traction: "If God wanted to forgive our sins, why not just forgive them"?[10] Presumably, God could just decree it—except for this factor: he is holy, just, and true. He must uphold the terms of the covenants. Therefore, he must judge treason and do so according to the stated terms of his covenants with our first parents in Eden, but also the Hebrew people at Sinai. His own law is not the enemy, but our treason renders us enemies (Romans 5:10). God must judge or cease to be God. But this is where the good news comes in, and it comes in the form of the Bible's teaching about *representation*.

By New Testament times there was a clear Jewish understanding of three things. First, that God was coming to reestablish his earthly rule through a promised Messiah, and, second, that Messiah's coming would lead to judgment of the great King's enemies and the enemies of his people. This was the message on the lips of Jesus (Mark 1:14–15), heralded as "good news" and calling for repentance. Third, it was also recognized that there was judgment after death followed by either the Age to Come (frequently referred to as "the Kingdom of

---

[10] Dawkins, *The God Delusion*, 253.

God," "kingdom of heaven," and "eternal life") or exclusion.[11] Where the doctrine of representation comes in is with the notion of Messiah, the anointed king of Israel.

The true King of Israel was God. So if God chose to anoint a king over Israel, he was having them fulfill a role of double representation: that of the true King, God, but also of Israel. Just as the Secretary of State represents the President of the United States before other nations and the President represents the people of the United States, so much more the king of Israel. When the anointed king comes he does so imaging forth the great King's (the Father's) image, not only possessing the word of God upon his heart but literally as the Word of God (John 1:14) and, at the same time, in the Adamic capacity as "the son of God" on earth, the heir of the kingdom. Adam gives way to Israel as God's son in the history of redemption. Israel is called to represent the representative of all people, Adam, but commits egregious treason too. Thus, the Son of God comes simultaneously to fulfill the covenant obligations of humanity (both in Adam and Israel) and the promises of God to uphold the covenants, including the pledge made to Adam and Noah to redeem his earthly kingdom and its citizens. The covenants made with Abraham and king David makes it specific—the Messiah will be a son of Abraham and a royal descendant of David. The Son of David is the Son of God, Jesus the Christ (Matthew 1:17).

The identification of the great King and the anointed crown prince is a one-to-one correspondence. The crown prince (Jesus as Israel—"the prince that prevails with God") represents the Father and therefore has authority to speak and act on the great King's behalf just as if he were the Father, so much so that Jesus could say: "Whoever has seen me has seen the Father. . . . The word that you hear is not mine but the Father's who sent me" (John 14:9, 24).

At the same time, Jesus' representation of Israel consists of his fulfilling covenant obligations of obedience but also bearing the

---

[11] I. Howard Marshall, "The New Testament Does Not Teach Universal Salvation," in *Universal Salvation? The Current Debate*, ed. Robin A. Parry and Christopher H. Partridge (Grand Rapids: Eerdmans, 2003), 56.

penalty for disobedience. Because the King has committed no treason, that is, he is without sin in his fulfilling of the will of the Father, only he can say on behalf of Israel (the people who represent the peoples of the world) "I always do the things that are pleasing to [the Father]" (John 8:29). And so the Father makes this public declaration about Jesus: "You are my beloved Son; with you I am well pleased" (Mark 1:11). This was never said of anyone before Jesus, not of Adam, not of Moses, not of Israel, not even of David; only Jesus. No other person in any other religion can make such a claim and substantiate it by tethering it to a historical event—the resurrection—in order to vindicate this amazing claim. Only Jesus therefore is holy and righteous, not just for himself, but for all those he represents—his people Israel. And even Israel, now that the covenant is fulfilled, may be reconstituted, which is what Jesus does by engrafting the Gentiles (whom he represented in the covenant made with humankind in Adam by coming as the last Adam; see 1 Corinthians 15:45). Only Jesus could represent *all* humanity in covenant with God. Only Jesus is qualified and capable to redeem humanity as our representative King.

But there is more; with the law fulfilled and Jesus preserved in perfect righteousness and holiness for his people, he now undertakes to remove their sin, guilt, and unrighteousness, beginning with providing perfect representative repentance. Jesus repents for his people by undergoing John's "baptism of repentance" (Mark 1:4). A perfect apology is issued on behalf of sinful people by a sinless king. Only Jesus could do this, and it met with the public approbation of the Father, who representatively endows Jesus with the inheritance of the divine life: "the Holy Spirit descended on him in bodily form, like a dove" (Luke 3:22). Only Jesus possesses the Holy Spirit without measure that he may give of the Spirit without limit.

Climactically, Jesus paid the price of treason for his people on the cross. "For our sake he made him to be sin who knew no sin, so that in him we might become the righteousness of God" (2 Corinthians 5:21). Since Jesus was without sin of his own he could, of his own accord, take the sin, guilt, and unrighteousness of his people and be condemned on their behalf. In this, the terms of the covenant are fulfilled and so a new covenant may be established. Jesus the King promises as much when he institutes a new covenant in his blood for the remission of sins and the gift of the Holy Spirit. On the cross the King comes into his kingdom: this is the nature of God's rule on earth—extending pardon to all those who are "in Christ" (Romans 3:24). The King reigns and he does so with love, mercy, and peace. Only Jesus was without treason, so only Jesus could voluntarily take the penalty for sin on behalf of others. This is why Jesus is the only way, and why he said so himself: "I am the way, and the truth, and the life. No one comes to the Father except through me" (John 14:6).

With his resurrection and ascension Jesus is hailed as the world's rightful King and vindicated in all he said and did. He inherits the earthly kingdom from his Father. Jesus rules and reigns, and he does so through the kingdom of God now being manifested on earth through love, mercy, peace, and grace. Now the King busies himself with applying the spoils of his great victory over God's true enemies of sin, guilt, death, and the evil one. He urgently applies his accomplished redemption through very personal, very specific means with haste. There is urgency in the mission of the King: for whereas in former times of ignorance "God overlooked" our treason until sin could be dealt with, "now he commands all people everywhere to repent, because he has fixed a day on which he will judge the world in righteousness by a man whom he has appointed; and of this he has given assurance to all by raising him from the dead" (Acts 17:30–31). The day of grace and forbearance of Christ's rule will have an end and all those who abide in treason against the Son will themselves bear the judgment of the Last Day when it will be too late.

THE GREAT COMMISSION

Now there is an urgency to evangelize the world because the Father of the reigning Son requires all to repent and embrace the *present* rule of the King—the way of the cross and resurrection, the way of reconciliation. And so in Matthew 28:18–20 we find Jesus the King speaking with full imperial authority, issuing forth his regal decree and commissioning his royal ambassadors to make haste in their task to image-forth his presence, speak his word, and do his actions in the application of his great work of redemption as he repossesses his Father's once-usurped kingdom, beginning with the souls of humankind.

Critical for understanding the "Great Commission" is the Jewish concept of *shelichim*, where the rabbinic proverb "the messenger of a man is as the man himself" obtains. Persons commissioned as *shelichim* were endowed with authority to legally and morally represent their commissioner. As Robert Scrudieri notes, "When the *shelichim* went on a mission, they were actually considered to be the person or group who sent them."[12] This concept of authoritative personal representation is brought directly into the New Testament understanding of the great commission but with two important innovations by Jesus: First, he commissioned apostles for missional endeavors even to the Gentiles, whereas the Old Testament *shelichim* never eclipsed the boundaries of the Jewish community; and second, the power of the commissioner (that is, the Holy Spirit sent by the Father and the Son) would actually be present with the commissioned to achieve the commissioning and its purposes. Thus, so far from abandoning those outside of the New Covenant in Christ, the Lord comes to them in person in the persons of those who are to love them as well.

In the Great Commission of Matthew 28:18–20 it is really the King himself who is engaging all nations with the Gospel. Only he has the authority to forgive, grant righteousness, and cleanse from unrighteousness, therefore only he possesses salvation. It is *God's* mission for only God has the power to forgive sins (cf. Luke 5:21), and he does so because he loves the world with the love a father has for his children (John 3:16). This is the *why* of the great commission. God must be present in Christ through his apostles if forgiveness is to be applied and reconciliation is to result in our being joint heirs with Christ by adoption as sons (Romans 8:17). And so the reclamation of God's earthly kingdom begins and it must do so in conjunction with

---

[12] Robert J. Scrudieri, *The Apostolic Church: One, Holy, Catholic and Missionary* (Chino, CA: Lutheran Society for Missiology, 1995), 9.

the apostolic commissioning of John 20:21–23, which ultimately gives way to the only way disciples are made in Matthew 28:18–20, namely through God's specific means of grace. In this way, God is the ultimate doer of the great commission. In this way also is he known and present with and for those he seeks to save. It is not merely a declaration of pardon (which God could have done anywhere); union with Christ, the holiness and righteousness of Christ, given in faith through the means of grace are necessary for salvation. The means of grace shift the focus from the now distant "once and for all" accomplishment that took place outside the walls of Jerusalem some two thousand years ago onto the present presence and activity of God applying redemption through disclosed means of grace. The King's urgency is the church's urgency for it is the King who works and is present with grace through the means-of-grace bearing church.

But because of their circumstances not all people have heard the good news. Shouldn't their circumstantial unbelief be excused since the means of God have not reached them? Actually, culpability falls back on humanity. All bear the guilt of high treason by participating in and perpetuating self-contrived rule (be it through religious beliefs or not). So highly prized is self-rule, by whatever form it appears, that the truth about the world's rightful sovereign is willfully exchanged for a lie, and thus God's judgment is just (Romans 1:18–32); yet all the while he labors to bring the Gospel of divine pardon to them.

What is more, one must be circumspect about what God has already done in his urgency to bring the Gospel to the entire world. In most cases, the Gospel has already been present but rejected, or once-embraced and then willfully discarded. In the first century the urgency of God brought the Gospel to Africa, the Subcontinent, throughout Europe and Asia. It is erroneous to say that Christianity is now coming to the Southern hemisphere or China; it was there for many hundreds of years before being purged by Islam, the resurgence of Confucianism, political ideology, and the like. Indeed, Philip Jenkins persuasively argues that the truth is that the modern missionary movement is part of a *return* of the Gospel to Africa, India, and China.[13]

To be sure, there are impediments to the spread of the Gospel. But God cannot be held responsible for the obstacles we placed in the way of his rescue. Though he pursues through a particular people and with particular means, humanity has presented the greatest encumbrances. In the early centuries of God's urgent pursuit the testimony of Acts 13–20 and Romans 1 shows the resolute allegiance of peoples to false religions. Persecutions, slander, alienation—the church endured many hardships though it bore good news for all people. Likewise in the succeeding centuries, sloth, inertia, greed, and the politicization of the church, where the kingdom of God was perverted into the so-called Holy Roman Empire, stultified God's Gospel endeavors. From the Enlightenment through today the malaise of the fairness doctrine, replete with tolerance ethics and political correctness, has stymied even the church's zeal to proclaim the Gospel. There are consequences to ideological allegiances, foremost of which is that they impede the King's pursuit of all and the personal application of the redemption he has won. Human sinfulness and the consequences of ideas lock people groups into systems of high treason. Humanity is to be faulted for humanity's plight. The Lord brings the solution. We set up obstacles.

CONCLUSION

The issue at play in the biblical narrative is not fairness but righteousness. Christian particularism is no more scandalous than specifically identifying the remedy for a universal ailment. The Lord saw that our bondage and blindness was so great that unless he, in his great love, came born of a woman, born under the law, we would be

---

[13] Philip Jenkins, *The Next Christendom: The Coming of Global Christianity* (Oxford and New York: Oxford University Press, 2002), 36, *et passim*. See also his *The Lost History of Christianity: The Thousand-Year Golden Age of the Church in the Middle East, Africa, and Asia—and How It Died* (San Francisco: HarperOne, 2008).

lost. The ailment is guilty unholiness, the result of high treason; the remedy is the righteous Anointed King who, in his representation of all, bears for taking away the sin of the world and its guilt, and grants us his holiness, a place in his gracious kingdom. It is this Jesus, the real Jesus of Israel's covenants and Scriptures, interpreted by his first followers in their light, and in turn the key to those Scriptures, whose name is the only name given under heaven whereby we may be saved. For only he can and has stood in our place.

Christ is the cure for sin, guilt, judgment, and death because no one could fulfill our collective obligations in covenant with God except a king who represented his people in holiness, righteousness, and propitiatory atonement before God. And since only Jesus passed through the grave, coming out the other side and returning to us, only he can be said to be the victor over death, only he can be the way, the truth, and the life (John 14:6). Only he can speak with knowledge and authority about divine judgment, the resurrection of the body, and everlasting life. For only he has been vindicated in his claims to be Israel's king and therefore the world's rightful Lord, the only one who has all authority in heaven and on earth, to speak for all, to act for all, to lay claim to all, to rule over all. The Father has vindicated him alone by way of the resurrection. It is the Father's hallmark that took place right in the fullness of time as a phenomenological event, which testifies that only Jesus mediates peace between God and humanity (Hebrews 9:15–28). Christ alone accomplished it; and by faith alone, received through the means of grace alone, he urgently applies it as a specified and personal act of love. There is news, good news, to herald from the battlefield of Golgotha: Christ has got the victory. Sin and death and judgment and the devil have been swallowed up, not only for the Jew but also the Gentile, for there is no other name given under heaven whereby we may be saved.

FOR FURTHER READING

Carson, Donald A. *The Gagging of God: Christianity Confronts Pluralism*. Grand Rapids: Zondervan, 1996.

Clifford, Paul Rowntree. *The Reality of the Kingdom: Making Sense of God's Reign in a World Like Ours*. Grand Rapids: Eerdmans, 1996.

Copan, Paul. *Is God a Moral Monster? Making Sense of the Old Testament God*. Grand Rapids: Baker, 2011.

Craig, William Lane. "Politically Incorrect Salvation" in *Christian Apologetics in the Modern World*, Timothy R. Phillips and Dennis L. Okholm, eds. Downers Grove, IL: InterVarsity, 1995, 75–97.

Hunter, Baker. *The End of Secularism*. Wheaton: Crossway, 2009.

Keller, Timothy. *The Reason for God: Belief in an Age of Skepticism*. New York: Dutton, 2008.

Newbigin, Leslie. *The Gospel in a Pluralist Society*. Grand Rapids: Eerdmans, 1989.

Ryken, Philip Graham. *Is Jesus the Only Way?* Wheaton: Crossway, 1999.

Wells, David F. *Above All Earthly Powers: Christ in the Postmodern World*. Grand Rapids: Eerdmans, 2005.

Wright, N. T. *The New Testament and the People of God, Christian Origins and the Question of God*, vol. 1. Minneapolis: Fortress Press, 1992.

_____. *The Resurrection of the Son of God, Christian Origins and the Question of* God, vol. 3. Minneapolis: Fortress Press, 2003.

6

GRATUITOUS EVIL
AND A GOD OF LOVE

Angus Menuge

INTRODUCTION

Everyone has heard of the problem of evil. If God is all-powerful (omnipotent), all-knowing (omniscient), and perfectly good, why is there any evil in the world? Since God is omniscient, we cannot suppose that some evil simply escapes his attention. Since God is omnipotent, he could also prevent any evil from occurring. And since he is perfectly good, many suppose he would want to prevent evil. But if God knows about all evil, has the power to prevent it and wants to do so, there would be no evil. But there is. So, the skeptic claims, either there is no God, or he is not omniscient, or he is not omnipotent, or he is not perfectly good. In addition to atheism, the other three skeptical alternatives have been embraced by some scholars. For open theists, the future is indefinite and not knowable even by God;[1] Rabbi Harold Kushner famously denied that God is really omnipotent;[2] and those philosophers known as Ockhamists claim that "God is good" is unintelligible, because we cannot use the human category of goodness to describe God at all.[3] But none of these maneuvers is compatible with orthodox Christianity. The standard response to the problem of evil, then, is that there are good reasons why an omniscient, omnipotent, and perfectly good God would permit evil.

Among the orthodox, there are several different kinds of response to the problem of evil. Proponents of a *theodicy* (a vindication of God) claim to know God's justification for allowing evil: some

---

[1] Defenders of open theism include Clark Pinnock, William Hasker, and many others. For an accessible statement of the view see Gregory A. Boyd, *God of the Possible: A Biblical Introduction to the Open View of God* (Grand Rapids, MI: Baker, 2000).

[2] Harold Kushner, *When Bad Things Happen to Good People* (New York: Schocken, 1981).

[3] For a discussion of C. S. Lewis's critique of Ockhamism, see David Baggett, "Is Divine Iconoclast as Bad as Cosmic Vivisectionist?" in *C. S. Lewis as Philosopher*, ed. David Baggett, Gary Habermas, and Jeff Walls (Downers Grove, IL: InterVarsity, 2008), 115–30.

greater good he wants to achieve. Others find theodicies presumptuous and implausible, but will offer a *defense*, which shows merely that there are plausible, possible justifications for God's permission of evil. Lastly, one can give a *narration* of evil, which rejects the attempt to justify God's permission of evil, but instead provides a coherent story showing how God works through evil to bring us to him.

In the literature, two different versions of the problem of evil have emerged. The *logical* problem asks: are God and evil consistent? The *evidential* problem, raised by William Rowe, is more modest: is God's existence probable given the evil observed in the world? We will first examine the logical problem of evil and the classic free will defense. Most philosophers, including Rowe, accept the force of the free will defense, but doubt that it provides a plausible account of all the evil in the world. Rowe points to examples of apparently "gratuitous" or pointless evil, not explained by free will or any other good. So we next examine Rowe's case and major lines of response. We then argue that some responses to Rowe are inadequate because they are preoccupied with God's *moral* justification for permitting evil. This overlooks God's primary aim, which is not the development of moral character, but saving sinners from a fallen world. We conclude by sketching a better response to Rowe: a narration of evil as found in the cross of Christ. This shows that our God is a God of love without developing detailed rationales for evil.

THE LOGICAL PROBLEM OF EVIL
AND THE FREE WILL DEFENSE

The logical problem of evil requires and explanation of how the existence of an omnipotent, omniscient, perfectly good God is consistent with the existence of evil. The best-known response to this problem is the Free Will Defense of Alvin Plantinga. Plantinga argues that God may be justified in allowing moral evil because if his creatures have morally significant free will then it must be possible for them to do evil, and a world with free creatures that also contains evil is more valuable than a world without both evil and free will.[4]

There are several well-known challenges to the free-will defense. Some argue that God could have given us free will but still ensured that we only made morally good choices. These thinkers subscribe to a theory of free will called *soft determinism*, according to which free will and determinism (the claim that every event has a cause) are compatible. On this view, a free choice is not one that is uncaused, but rather one that is caused in the right way. If all our choices were ultimately caused by a good God, then they would be caused in the right way, and hence free, but those choices could not be evil. However, soft determinism does not account for the moral responsibility of human beings. This is because any choice the agent makes is ultimately caused by factors outside of the agent's control, so there is no reason to say that the agent is any more responsible than these factors for the action. As Robert Kane has argued, soft determinism fails to ground the idea that "genuinely free agents must have 'ultimate' or 'buck-stopping' responsibility for their free actions and character."[5] If soft determinism were true, we would be like computers programmed by God to do good. For genuine responsibility, one needs *libertarian* free will, where the choice originates with the agent. So if genuine responsibility is sufficiently valuable, God is justified in creating people with libertarian free will. But not even God can make people with libertarian free will make good choices, since the choices are up to them.

Most critics concede that free will makes moral evil possible. But they want to know why the physical and mental consequences of

---

[4] Alvin Plantinga, "God, Evil and the Metaphysics of Freedom," in *The Problem of Evil*, ed. Marilyn McCord Adams and Robert Merrihew Adams (New York: Oxford University Press, 1990), 83–109. Originally published in Alvin Plantinga, *The Nature of Necessity* (Oxford: Clarendon Press, 1974), 164–93.

[5] Robert Kane, "Free Will: The Elusive Ideal," *Philosophical Studies* 75 (1994): 25–60, 33. With kind permission from Springer Science+Business Media.

wrong choices are so bad. It certainly seems conceivable that God could create a world in which morally wrong choices do not have such bad effects. We can imagine a sort of "flight simulator world," in which one can choose to shoot someone, but the bullets emerge as harmless marshmallows.[6] Yet if moral responsibility is something valuable to God, such a world is less valuable than our own, since its people avoid facing the bad consequences of their choices. What is more, this would not be good for them: if people do not have to confront the impact of evil choices, it is likely that their souls would become even more infested with hatred, anger, lust, envy, vanity and pride. As evidence, consider the meanness, scorn, and obscenity found in anonymous internet postings about politically sensitive issues.

C. S. Lewis further argued that if God values a community of free souls, then there must be a common world in which they act, and the independence of this world from any of the souls makes suffering possible. Such a world is required so that souls can distinguish themselves from each other and communicate.[7] For example, if I am to distinguish your voice from one in my head, we need to be separated from each other in some shared medium, such as space; and if you speak to me, there needs to be a medium of communication, such as the air that transmits the sound waves to my ear. Yet, in order for us to reliably act, these mediums must be governed by stable laws, so that, for example, we do not have to tie down our car in case it ascends into space. Responsible choices presuppose not only free will, but a world in which the consequences of our choices are predictable. But then, if we make bad choices (either immoral or imprudent ones), these same laws will lead to bad effects. The same gravity that keeps my car on the slab will also accelerate the statue heaved off the parapet to the Earl below, and it may also kill me if I

---

[6] The example is from Jerry Root, "C. S. Lewis and the Problem of Evil," in *C. S. Lewis: Lightbearer in the Shadowlands*, ed. Angus Menuge (Wheaton, IL: Crossway, 1997), 353–66, 360.

[7] C. S. Lewis, *The Problem of Pain* (New York: Macmillan, 1962), ch. 2.

jump with an old bungee cord. So, it is plausible that in any world orderly enough for free action, suffering is possible.[8]

Still, if a responsible world is such a dangerous world, some will argue that free will is not worth the price in terms of the amount and degree of horrendous suffering it causes. This objection can partly be answered by examining more closely why it is we value free will so much. We are creatures, made to be dependent on God, and God surely did not grant us free will merely because he valued personal autonomy. After all, we might choose to turn our world into a hell on earth and to consign ourselves to eternal damnation by rejecting God's grace. A more plausible answer is that God values creaturely free will, not for its own sake, but because it is a necessary precondition for love, which is inherently valuable. God wants us to be loving sons, not slaves, but love cannot be compelled. Jerry Root recounts the example of a doll called "Chatty Cathy," which repeated "I love you" when a cord was pulled.[9] The doll cannot love, and making it more intelligent would not change that fact. While fallen creatures are God's enemies, incapable of loving God on their own power, through grace, the new man in Christ can begin to love God. Since we cannot be compelled to accept such grace (we can reject the gift), and only grace makes love possible, love cannot exist without free will.

THE EVIDENTIAL PROBLEM OF EVIL

William Rowe calls attention to two kinds of evil which appear gratuitous in the sense that they are not obviously required to allow any greater good, including morally significant free will. The first

---

[8] In the same vein, T. J. Mawson argues plausibly that the possibility of some natural evil is inevitable in a world in which people have conflicting desires and choose to pursue their interests at each other's expense. For example, if two people are in the desert and one pursues his interest by drinking the last water, the other suffers the natural evil of dehydration. See T. J. Mawson, "The Possibility of a Free-will Defence for the Problem of Natural Evil," *Religious Studies* 40 (2004): 23–42.

[9] Jerry Root, "C. S. Lewis and the Problem of Evil," 360.

kind includes natural evils that are not directly the result of human choices and which have no obvious effect on humans. Rowe's famous example is a fawn trapped in a forest fire: the fawn is severely burned and dies after several days of agony, but no human ever knows of its plight, and so could not be made better (e.g., more compassionate) as a result.[10] The second kind of case includes events that do result from free will but which seem gratuitously horrendous. Rowe's (actual) example is a five-year old girl who was raped, beaten and killed by her mother's boyfriend.[11] Surely there could have been plenty of morally significant choices without anyone suffering that. Rowe has developed several different versions of the evidential argument from evil, and he is aware that his argument cannot move theists who have strong independent reasons for believing in God (in that sense he defends a "friendly atheism"). But he claims that the atheist who lacks (or doubts) these reasons can defend his unbelief as follows:

1. Probably, there are pointless evils (e.g., the fawn's suffering).

2. If God exists, there are no pointless evils, therefore,

3. Probably, God does not exist.[12]

Many potential responses to Rowe are inconclusive. In defending the scope of his free will defense, Plantinga points out that natural evil (which would include the fawn's suffering) may be the result of the free choices of non-human persons, such as Satan and his minions.[13] But all Plantinga is hoping to show is that God is logically consistent with natural evil, which Rowe grants. Rowe's claim is

---

[10] William Rowe, "The Problem of Evil and Some Varieties of Atheism," *American Philosophical Quarterly* 16 (1979): 335–41, 337.

[11] William Rowe, "Ruminations About Evil," *Philosophical Perspectives 5: Philosophy of Religion* (1991): 70–88, 72.

[12] William Rowe, "Friendly Atheism, Skeptical Theism, and the Problem of Evil," *International Journal for Philosophy of Religion* 59 (2006): 79–92, 80. With kind permission from Springer Science+Business Media.

[13] Alvin Plantinga, "God, Evil and the Metaphysics of Freedom," 108.

merely that apparently gratuitous evil makes God's existence improbable, and it would be a long and difficult task to provide evidence of demonic activity in the world. Again, according to the Bible's account, the primal sin of Adam and Eve in disobeying God's command not to eat of the tree of the knowledge of good and evil resulted in a cosmic Fall (Romans 8:20–22). What we call natural evil is the effect of the curse (Genesis 3:16–19), which traces back to human choices. However, this answer is hard to defend in our contemporary milieu, since many accept the standard scientific picture of an old earth and an animal kingdom red in tooth and claw before human beings came on the scene.[14] And this answer does not tell us why God allows the curse to *continue* to cause suffering.

When we turn to Rowe's second kind of case, some think that as tragic as the girl's fate was, the mother's boyfriend did have the morally significant ability to make better choices, but simply failed to do so, and so perhaps the value of free will does at least explain even such terrible suffering. However, D. Z. Phillips worries that the free will defense fails to account for cases in which free will seems irrelevant because all of a person's options involve horrendous evil. A famous, fictional but entirely realistic example is "Sophie's choice," an impossible choice presented to Sophie Zawitoska, a Polish survivor of Auschwitz.[15] In the story, an SS officer told Sophie that both her children (Jan and Eva) would be gassed unless she chose one to live, thereby assuring the death of the other child. She chose to save Jan at the expense of Eva, but remained tormented by the evil

---

[14] One recent attempt to reconcile standard science with the cosmic fall is proposed by William Dembski in his *The End of Christianity: Finding God in an Evil World* (Nashville, TN: B&H Academic, 2009). Dembski argues that since God is outside time and yet knows everything that happens in time, human actions can affect the world retroactively. Just as God, knowing from eternity that you would pray about a time after it occurred, could still answer that prayer, so, knowing from eternity that man would fall, God might curse the creation retroactively.

[15] William Styron, *Sophie's Choice* (New York: Random House, 1979). The example is discussed in D. Z. Phillips, *The Problem of Evil and the Problem of God* (Minneapolis, MN: Fortress Press, 2005), 41–43.

choice until she committed suicide. Phillips argues that even if free will explains why evil in general exists, it does not explain or justify the particular evils that occur or the degradation they cause. He points out that there is no "*logical link* between the requirement that some evils have to exist if goods are to exist and the *actual* evils which do exist."[16] Why after all, did Sophie have to make *that* choice? Why do there have to be any choices confined to morally abhorrent options? Would not the world still be morally significant without such horrendous choices? Suppose, for example, that Sophie had been offered the chance to save both children if she agreed to have one hand amputated. Would not her costly agreement to this horrible demand still have had the highest moral significance? But Sophie was not given any noble options.

OUR COGNITIVE LIMITATIONS

One of the stronger lines of reply to Rowe calls attention to human cognitive limitations: finite, fallen creatures are not well-placed to discern whether or not an omniscient God has a reason to permit evil, so we cannot reasonably claim that some evil is probably pointless. Stephen Wykstra points out that appeal to apparently pointless evil only has force if it is reasonable to suppose that we would be able to see the point of the evil if it had one. If there appears to be no dog in the room, this is good reason to think no dog is there, but the fact that we cannot see sand-fleas is no reason to deny their presence. In Wykstra's terms, sand-fleas have low "seeability" for creatures like us. But so do God's reasons for allowing many particular evils.

> A modest proposal would be that his wisdom is to ours, roughly as an adult human's is to a one-month old infant's. ... But if outweighing goods ... exist in connection with instances of suffering, that we should discern most of them seems about as likely as that a one-month old should discern

---

[16] D. Z. Phillips, *The Problem of Evil and the Problem of God*, 55.

most of his parents' purposes for those pains they allow him to suffer—which is to say, it is not likely at all.[17]

Kirk Durston gives further support by noting our inability to discern the complex causal consequences of events.[18] The consequences of a single event may grow exponentially because the event influences a large network of interconnected causal chains. For example, had his mother adopted a different sleeping position on the night Winston Churchill was conceived, this would have affected the pathways of the spermatozoa and hence the resulting zygote so that the person we know as Sir Winston Churchill would never have lived, with potentially major ramifications for World War II.[19] Had Winston's mother been more restless, the world might have fallen to Nazism! Durston argues with some rigor that since changing a single event affects all of a vast number of interconnected causal chains, we simply cannot know or even reliably estimate what the world would have been like if an event had not happened. As a result, it is impossible to reasonably claim that the world would have been better if the fawn had not been burned or if the girl had not been raped and killed.

In the case of the fawn, the response to Rowe can be further strengthened by pointing out that amongst our cognitive limitations is the fact that we do not know what it is like to be a fawn, and the behavioral evidence provides no good reason to think it has consciousness of itself as an individual persisting across time, which

---

[17] Stephen Wykstra, "The Humean Obstacle to Evidential Arguments From Suffering: On Avoiding the Evils of 'Appearance'," in *The Problem of Evil*, ed. Marilyn McCord Adams and Robert Merrihew Adams, 138–60, 155–56. This essay was originally published in *International Journal for Philosophy of Religion* 16 (1984): 73–93. With kind permission from Springer Science+Business Media.

[18] Kirk Durston, "The Consequential Complexity of History and Gratuitous Evil," *Religious Studies* 36 (2000): 65–80.

[19] Kirk Durston, "The Consequential Complexity of History and Gratuitous Evil," 65–66.

at the very least would make its suffering much less than our own.[20] When we suffer, we are also aware that we have suffered and may suffer further. At the height of the grieving process, C. S. Lewis observed, we may "not only live each endless day in grief, but live each day thinking about living each day in grief."[21]

The appeal to our cognitive limitations effectively blocks Rowe's argument,[22] but it does not overcome the sense of individual injustice done to the girl, or explain why people like Lewis must suffer so much grief. While the critics of Rowe show that we cannot know that any evils are probably pointless, this does not provide a plausible account of what the point of apparently gratuitous evil might be, or answer the nagging objection that an omnipotent God should have been able to achieve the same good end in a different way, so that the evil did not occur. Merely blocking Rowe's arguments leads only to a stalemate between theism and atheism.

This has led to a couple of further responses to Rowe. One approach is to emphasize the positive philosophical and scientific case for theism. The stronger our arguments for a good God, the more confidence we have that there must be a reason for apparently pointless evils even though we do not know what it is. This approach is particularly powerful when atheism and theism are compared directly, for it can be argued that atheism cannot justify features of reality required to state the problem of evil. According to the *argument from reason*, were the atheist correct that nature is all there is, "we could never muster a sufficient reason for thinking that our

---

[20] C. S. Lewis develops this point in his chapter on "Animal Pain," in his *The Problem of Pain*, 131–33.

[21] C. S. Lewis, *A Grief Observed* (New York: Bantam Books, 1976), 9.

[22] Further good parries for specific formulations of Rowe's arguments are provided by James Beilby, "Does the Empirical Problem of Evil Prove that Theism is Improbable?" *Religious Studies* 32 (1996): 315–23, and Jeff Jordan, "Blocking Rowe's New Evidential Argument from Evil," *Religious Studies* 37 (2001): 435–49.

belief-forming mechanisms were in fact reliable."[23] This is because natural selection is only interested in useful beliefs and reasoning (beliefs and reasoning which produce adaptive behaviors). But useful beliefs do not need to be mostly true: so long as one's body avoids lions, it does not matter if one believes they are friendly. And useful arguments need not be sound (it might be very useful to argue that all teenagers are incapable of driving safely!). But the atheist's evidential argument from evil attempts to influence our beliefs by reason, which is pointless if our beliefs and reason are unreliable.[24]

Apologist Ravi Zacharias goes further and points out that the atheist has difficulty in justifying the existence of evil itself.[25] For example, the philosopher J. L. Mackie claimed evil as a reason to deny God's existence, but then argued that an objective moral law was incredible because it could only be explained by a divine lawgiver.[26] Yet if there is no objective moral law, nothing counts as objectively evil, and the atheist cannot then produce evil as data that needs to be explained. Richard Dawkins admits as much when he claims that "The universe we observe has precisely the properties we should expect if there is, at the bottom, no design, no purpose, no evil and no good,"[27] though he contradicts himself by insisting that human beings should promote generosity and altruism to counteract our

---

[23] Ed Martin, "Planting a Rawlsian Garden: Proper Function, the Problem of Evil, and 'Thinking Behind the Veil'," in *Tough-Minded Christianity: Honoring the Legacy of John Warwick Montgomery*, ed. William Dembski and Thomas Schirrmacher (Nashville, TN: B&H, 2008), 558–96, 589.

[24] For more details, see my "Beyond Skinnerian Creatures: A Defense of the Lewis/Plantinga Critique of Evolutionary Naturalism," *Philosophia Christi* 5 (2003): 143–65.

[25] Ravi Zacharias, "Is God the Source of My Suffering?" in his *Jesus Among Other Gods* (Nashville, TN: Thomas Nelson, 2002), 103–39.

[26] J. L. Mackie, *The Miracle of Theism: Arguments For and Against the Existence of God* (Oxford: Clarendon Press, 1982), 115.

[27] Richard Dawkins, *River Out of Eden: A Darwinian View of Life* (New York: Basic Books, 1995), 133.

innate selfishness,[28] a moral intuition which assumes the objective good and evil he has denied.

A second way to rebut Rowe is to identify a general reason beyond free will which can explain why God allows his creatures to continue suffering from the curse. The most popular answer involves God's concern for our souls.

SOUL-MAKING

The soul-making theory finds support in many passages of scripture.[29] C. S. Lewis calls our attention to four important examples.[30] Jeremiah compares Israel, and by extension all of humanity, to clay in the hand of a potter (Jeremiah 18). The clay is resistant to the potter's designs and is "spoiled in the potter's hand," just as we fell into sin by rebelling against our creator's intentions. Out of love, the potter reshapes us "into another vessel, as it seemed good to the potter to do" (Jeremiah 18:4), just as God calls the new man in Christ to be re-created "after the likeness of God in true righteousness and holiness" (Ephesians 4:22–24; see also Colossians 3:9–10). Since fallen creatures are by nature enemies of God, this reshaping is painful: it is not only against the grain of our will, but it involves a kind of death, the mortification of the old Adam. As Lewis realized, the more God loves us, the more this process is going to hurt:

> One can imagine a sentient picture, after being rubbed and scraped and re-commenced for the tenth time, wishing that it were only a thumb-nail sketch whose making was over in a minute . . . but then we are wishing not for more love but for less.[31]

---

[28] Richard Dawkins, *The Selfish Gene* (New York: Oxford University Press, 1976), 2–3.

[29] This approach was pushed to the forefront by John Hick's *Evil and the God of Love* (New York: Harper & Row, 1966; revised 1978).

[30] C. S. Lewis, *The Problem of Pain*, 42–47.

[31] C. S. Lewis, *The Problem of Pain*, 42–43.

Later in his career, after losing his wife to cancer, Lewis came to realize that a divine surgeon who will stop at nothing to improve our soul may allow us to suffer *more* than a cosmic vivisectionist who would soon discard us as failed experiments.[32] The great metaphysical poet, George Herbert, reached a similar conclusion:

Yet take Thy way; for sure, Thy way is best:
Stretch or contract me Thy poor debtor:
This is but tuning of the breast,
To make the music better.[33]

Scripture also compares our relation to God to the relation between sheep and shepherd. With weak eyesight and little understanding, the sheep has a much poorer idea than does the shepherd of what is good for it. The sheep may not enjoy being herded by dogs, confined in pens and going through pest removal, but all of these things are to its benefit. Likewise, humans blinded by sin and confused by their cognitive limitations may not enjoy being herded into their vocational responsibilities, confined by God's laws and enduring medical treatment, but all of these things are for their own true good.

A less metaphorical analogy is the relation between a son and his father (Hebrews 12:3–11). Just as our earthly father disciplines his children, so our heavenly Father "disciplines us for our good, that we may share his holiness." At the time, such discipline "seems painful rather than pleasant, but later it yields the peaceful fruit of righteousness to those who have been trained by it" (Hebrews 12:10–11). A loving Father will set limits, punish disobedience, and allow us to suffer some of the consequences of our own actions.

The closest analogy of all is a man's love for a woman (Ephesians 5:22–33). This analogy must be read in light of a biblical understanding of love, which is much more than mere kindness.

---

[32] C. S. Lewis, *A Grief Observed*, 49–50.

[33] George Herbert, "The Temper," in *The Works of George Herbert in Prose and Verse* (New York: John Wurtle Lovell, 1881), 138.

Christ's love for his bride, the church, means that his goal is to "sanctify her, having cleansed her by the washing of water with the word, so that he might present the church to himself in splendor, without spot or wrinkle or any such thing, that she might be holy and without blemish" (Ephesians 5:26–27). What this shows is that:

> Love, in its own nature, demands the perfecting of the beloved; that the mere "kindness" which tolerates anything except suffering in its object is, in that respect, at the opposite pole from Love. . . . Love may forgive all infirmities and love still in spite of then: but Love cannot cease to will their removal.[34]

As Lewis suggested through the character of Eustace Clarence Scrubb, a self-centered boy who became a dragon,[35] the process of divine cleaning is going to be painful for sinners who have encased their rebellious wills in many defensive layers.

While the scriptural basis for the soul-making theory seems incontestable, there are two different interpretations of God's primary objective in the soul-making process, which are often not carefully distinguished. On the first interpretation, God is primarily interested in improving the moral character of his creatures (call this the *moralistic soul-making theory*); on the second interpretation, while God does care about our moral character, he is most concerned with showing creatures their inability to save themselves and hence their need for an external savior (call this the *creaturely conviction soul-making theory*). I will defend the theological and philosophical superiority of the creaturely conviction approach.

THE MORALISTIC SOUL-MAKING THEORY

Two powerful exponents of the moralistic soul-making argument are Stewart Goetz and Richard Swinburne. Goetz presents a strict

---

[34] C. S. Lewis, *The Problem of Pain*, 46.

[35] C. S. Lewis, *The Voyage of the "Dawn Treader"* (New York: Macmillan, 1962).

theodicy, claiming to know why God allows suffering. He argues that "the purpose of life is to experience perfect or complete happiness,"[36] a happiness found only in heaven. However, in order for enjoyment of this happiness to be just, there must be a change in moral character: "the significant change in moral character that is a prerequisite for the experience of complete happiness comes about because of a choice ... the mental act of repentance." Goetz calls this choice a good-seeking self-forming choice.[37] Since this choice to turn away from evil is free, evil remains possible.

While Goetz's account is developed with great sophistication, Lutherans will discern a clear theological flaw. By making our good-seeking self-forming choice a prerequisite for enjoying heaven, Goetz appears committed to a decision theology, which is incompatible with Scripture's teaching of salvation by grace alone. Nothing we choose contributes to our salvation. Furthermore, Goetz says that "a person will justly experience complete happiness, *if* he chooses rightly."[38] But our salvation is not a matter of our being treated justly. The wages of sin is death (Romans 6:23), and we are saved not because it is our just deserts, but through the free gift of Christ's righteousness.[39] By making moral formation a prerequisite for salvation, Goetz's account appears to espouse works-righteousness.

A second limitation of Goetz's account is that it focuses almost exclusively on moral evil, saying very little about the natural evils we suffer (such as sickness, famines, and earthquakes). However, Richard Swinburne has developed many ingenious explanations. For example, he argues that "natural evil provides opportunities for

---

[36] Stewart Goetz, "The Argument from Evil," in *The Blackwell Companion to Natural Theology*, ed. William Lane Craig and J. P. Moreland (Malden, MA: Blackwell, 2009), 449–97, 458.

[37] Stewart Goetz, "The Argument from Evil," 465.

[38] Stewart Goetz, "The Argument from Evil," 469.

[39] For a powerful critique of salvation as a matter of "rights," see chapter 4 of C. S. Lewis's *The Great Divorce* (New York: Macmillan, 1946).

especially valuable kinds of emotional response and free choice,"[40] emphasizing the great goods of compassion, courage and sympathy. The general idea is that natural evil provides opportunities for greater moral goods, such as character development, moral responsibility, initiatives to change, and admirable responses to the suffering of ourselves and others.

Although there may be some truth in what Swinburne says, his account faces serious objections, as D. Z. Phillips has shown. For one thing, Swinburne's approach is morally objectionable because "the sufferings of others are made instrumental to the self,"[41] so that we could imagine a pious Christian congratulating a leper for providing such an excellent opportunity for compassion! Perversely, this makes it hard to see why the world would not be better with even more suffering, and hence more opportunities for compassion. Secondly, as Phillips points out, it is false that suffering always makes people morally better. The lecher may be spurred to cure his disease only to continue his debauchery. Depression may lead to suicide. Suffering brutal treatment, as in the Nazi concentration camps, may produce a few moral saints, but it usually degrades people, making them selfish, mean and petty.[42] If suffering has a point, it is not always the point of making someone morally better.

But, as Phillips argues, there are deeper problems with Swinburne's approach. The underlying rationale, common to many theodicies, is that evils can be morally justified by greater goods. This, however, assumes a tendentious moral theory, consequentialism, according to which an action is morally justified if it has good overall consequences. On this view, God is portrayed as a moral economist doing cost-benefit analysis on a cosmic spreadsheet: so long as the good column outweighs the evil column, God's

---

[40] Richard Swinburne, "The Problem of Evil," ch. 11 in his *The Existence of God*, second edition (New York: Oxford University Press, 2004), 236–72, 240. By permission of Oxford University Press.

[41] D. Z. Phillips, *The Problem of Evil and the Problem of God*, 59.

[42] Phillips discusses these and many other counter-examples of Swinburne in ch. 3 of his *The Problem of Evil and the Problem of God*.

management of the world is morally solvent. This picture does violence to the biblical understanding that God has fatherly concern for *each* of his creatures: he does not aim to trash the lives of some people merely to promote overall edification. It also seems to misunderstand providence. It is true that a loving God will work to produce good out of evil actions and circumstances (Genesis 50:20; Romans 8:28), but this is not the same as condoning (or worse, celebrating) evil, or permitting more fortunate creatures to do so, because of perceived opportunities to benefit from the suffering of others. Providence is a free response of grace and love, not an actuarial exercise in moral book-balancing. As Lewis emphasizes, the great good which God achieved through the crucifixion in no way justifies Judas' actions.[43] There is, after all, no reason to say that they had to happen: if Judas had not betrayed Jesus, God's will would have been done anyway, through some other means. In his providential work, God is not justifying evils, but loving us through and in spite of them (Romans 5:8).

Finally, it seems implausible that God's primary aim is to make us morally better using suffering as an obstacle course:

> The site of the obstacle course is strewn with corpses and casualties, and even among those who cross the line, no one has a perfect score. What was all this for? . . . So if we speak the language of theodicy, God invents a test for human life that he knows will not work.[44]

Suffering may improve some people, but it does not make anyone perfect or make them acceptable to God. Further, a person may become more morally upright by outward standards, yet, by depending on his own righteousness rather than the righteousness of Christ, he may spend an eternity in hell. Another person may be abominable in his earthly life, know it, and be saved by his faith in Christ's saving work. This argues that God's primary reason for allowing suffering is not moralistic at all.

---

[43] C. S. Lewis, *The Problem of Pain*, 111.

[44] D. Z. Phillips, *The Problem of Evil and the Problem of God*, 83.

THE CREATURELY CONVICTION SOUL-MAKING THEORY

Essential to a sound understanding of suffering is a recognition of the truth about us as God's creatures. The consequence of sin is that we live in an illusion of self-sufficiency, thinking that we can manage quite well by ourselves without God. One of the ways that God awakens us to our true condition is through pain:

> The creature's illusion of self-sufficiency must, for the creature's sake, be shattered; and by trouble or fear of trouble . . . God shatters it. . . . And this illusion . . . may be at its strongest in some very honest, kindly, and temperate people, and on such people, therefore, misfortune must fall.[45]

When God allows his creatures to suffer, it is not primarily because he has calculated some moral improvement that he can achieve for this life (although that may happen), but because he "desires all people to be saved and to come to the knowledge of the truth" (1 Timothy 2:4). Our sinful condition blinds us to the truth about our predicament, so that we rely on our own efforts to earn God's favor. Pain breaks this deceitful spell by shouting to us that we do not have our lives under control. When we cry out for help for ourselves or others, we confess our need for something beyond ourselves. As Ed Martin says, "one discovers through experiencing harsh evils that one's hope does not lie in oneself but must be outwardly directed."[46]

On this view, even if we cannot know it, we may as well agree with Rowe that there is *morally* gratuitous evil. Such evil is not especially "deserved" by its victims (John 9:3): in the sense in which it is deserved, we *all* deserve it (Luke 13:1–5). Nor is it allowed or inflicted *in order* to achieve a greater moral good, as if God's will would not have been done without it. We can admit that people in concentration camps and the five year old girl in Rowe's example suffered hideous evils which, for all we can tell, did not make the

---

[45] C. S. Lewis, *The Problem of Pain*, 97–98.

[46] Ed Martin, "Planting a Rawlsian Garden," 575.

world a better place, and which would not be "morally justified" if they had. What good came of these horrors depended entirely on the gracious providential *gifts* of God. In admitting this, we can avoid the kind of triumphalist theodicy which, as Phillips says, betrays people's suffering by misrepresenting it: "Betrayal occurs every time explanations and justifications of evils are offered which are simplistic, insensitive, incredible or obscene."[47] But in a world of such evil, all but the most willfully self-deceived can see that God's creatures and the whole creation are dependent on God.

While the creaturely conviction soul-making theory is a promising response to Rowe, it is incomplete. To understand the worst evils—horrendous, unjustified evils—we must focus more closely on the work of Christ.

A CHRISTOCENTRIC APPROACH

As Jeffrey Mallinson has argued, Lutheran theology affirms not only a theology of the cross, but an epistemology of the cross (a theory of knowledge which says we know God through Christ's work on the cross).[48] Unlike philosophical theism, which attempts to understand the divine by abstract reason, the epistemology of the cross insists that God is most clearly revealed in the person and work of the God-man, Jesus Christ, and especially in his suffering on our behalf. Theodicies and defenses are developed within the framework of a thin philosophical theism which provides little insight into who God is, how we have rebelled against him, and what he has done for us in loving response. For this kind of insight, we need a history of God's

---

[47] D. Z. Phillips, *The Problem of Evil and the Problem of God*, xi.

[48] Jeffrey Mallinson, "Epistemology of the Cross: A Lutheran Response to Philosophical Theisms," in *Theologia et Apologia*, ed. Adam Francisco, Korey Maas, and Steven Mueller (Eugene, OR: Wipf & Stock, 2007), 23–44.

interaction with humanity,[49] within which we can hope to find a *narration* of evil.[50]

Philosophical theism adopts an epistemology of glory, which begins with the greatness of God and sees evil as a difficulty to be rationalized. By contrast, an epistemology of the cross "does not *explain away* or try to show how particular instances of evil produce some greater good."[51] Rather, it *starts* with the evil and suffering found on the cross. On the cross we see a refutation of many glib theodicies and defenses, because Christ suffers wholly undeserved, unjustified, gratuitous, horrendous evil, and he does not do so primarily because he wants to make *this* world a better place, or merely to set us a moral example.

The cross embodies both Law and Gospel in the most powerful ways. On the Law side, we have an accurate depiction of the horrific load of sin which infects us all, and of the just punishment which it deserves. When we complain about the problem of evil, we would prefer to make it an external theoretical or political discussion, rather than an internal, personal problem that blinds us to its reality. Like a street urchin recruited into a terrorist militia, we are conceived in iniquity (Psalm 51:5) and our complicity with evil prevents us from seeing it clearly. For that, we must be confronted with the counter-perspective of a sinless outsider. In this bright light, evil cannot be contained in the tidy, coherent categories of a theodicy. This world is not a preparatory school for moral beings. It is a spiritual leper colony.

Yet, on the Gospel side, we see that Christ is not here not to punish us but to affirm his solidarity with fallen mankind (Hebrews 2:17–18; 4:15), bearing our sin, suffering every evil and taking the

---

[49] An excellent recent attempt to provide such a history which includes the whole framework of biblical history is N. T. Wright's *Evil and the Justice of God* (Downers Grove, IL: InterVarsity, 2006).

[50] See Paul Ricoeur, "Evil, a Challenge to Philosophy and Theology," in his *Figuring the Sacred: Religion, Narrative, and Imagination* (Minneapolis, MN: Fortress Press, 1995), 249–61, 251–52.

[51] Jeffrey Mallinson, "Epistemology of the Cross," 32.

full measure of wrath which we deserve (Isaiah 53). As Ed Martin notes, "There is an unquantifiable kinship of spirit that happens between those who have suffered in like manner."[52] This includes the most horrendous and gratuitous suffering that Rowe emphasizes, because it is only the one who has suffered evil who understands it. Ravi Zacharias concurs:

> *It is the woman who has been raped who understands what rape is, not the rapist. . . . It is only the One who died for our sins who can explain to us what evil is.*[53]

God does not answer the problem of evil by providing intellectually satisfying formulas. That would be appropriate if evil were a problem from which we were detached—like a problem in theoretical physics. Since evil is an immersive, existential condition, God answers by *actions* of love. His goal is not moral improvement, but to show us our true condition, our inability to save ourselves from that condition, and hence our absolute dependence on Christ for salvation. As Paul writes, "Wretched man that I am! Who will deliver me from this body of death? Thanks be to God through Jesus Christ our Lord!" (Romans 7:24–25).

Christ is God's answer to the problem of evil. Therefore, any apologetic for the problem of evil should not waste time in philosophical theisms which paint blurry pictures of who God is, who we are, and how we can be saved. It should be a defense focused on the historical case for Christ's crucifixion and resurrection. In this context, we see more clearly what evil is, what God has done about it, and what he will do. The resurrection of Christ's glorified, imperishable body also points to a final answer to evil, a new heaven and a new earth in which evil will have no dominion.

---

[52] Ed Martin, "Planting a Rawlsian Garden," 583–84.

[53] Ravi Zacharias, "Is God the Source of My Suffering?" 136, italics in original. Reprinted by permission. *Jesus Among Other Gods*, Ravi Zacharias, copyright © 2002, Thomas Nelson Inc. Nashville, Tennessee. All rights reserved.

CONCLUSION

Philosophical responses to the problem of evil are not without merit. They can show that evil and God are logically consistent, that human cognitive limitations make it impossible for Rowe to state a conclusive evidential argument from evil, and that atheism cannot account for the reliability of reason or the existence of evil on which the argument from evil depends. But theodicies and defenses run a terrible risk of falsifying the hard realities of human suffering and making of God a heartless moral accountant. Only in Christ's cross do we see the truth about ourselves and God's gracious and loving response. Only here can we face gratuitous, horrendous evil, and show Christ's suffering, with us and for us, as the answer of a loving God.

FOR FURTHER READING

Adams, Marilyn McCord and Robert Merrihew Adams, eds. *The Problem of Evil*. New York: Oxford University Press, 1990.

Baggett, David. "Is Divine Iconoclast as Bad as Cosmic Vivisectionist?" in *C. S. Lewis as Philosopher*, ed. David Baggett, Gary Habermas and Jeff Walls. Downers Grove, IL: InterVarsity, 2008, 115–30.

Beilby, James. "Does the Empirical Problem of Evil Prove that Theism is Improbable?" *Religious Studies* 32 (1996): 315–23.

Dembski, William. *The End of Christianity: Finding God in an Evil World*. Nashville, TN: B&H Academic, 2009.

Durston, Kirk. "The Consequential Complexity of History and Gratuitous Evil," *Religious Studies* 36 (2000): 65–80.

Goetz, Stewart. "The Argument From Evil," in *The Blackwell Companion to Natural Theology*, ed. William Lane Craig and J. P. Moreland. Malden, MA: Blackwell, 2009, 449–97.

Jordan, Jeff. "Blocking Rowe's New Evidential Argument from Evil," *Religious Studies* 37 (2001): 435–49.

Lewis, C. S. *The Problem of Pain*. New York: Macmillan, 1962.

Mallinson, Jeffrey. "Epistemology of the Cross: A Lutheran Response to Philosophical Theisms," in *Theologia et Apologia*, ed. Adam Francisco, Korey Maas and Steven Mueller. Eugene, OR: Wipf & Stock, 2007, 23–44.

Martin, Ed. "Planting a Rawlsian Garden: Proper Function, the Problem of Evil, and 'Thinking Behind the Veil'," in *Tough-Minded Christianity: Honoring the Legacy of John Warwick Montgomery*, ed. William Dembski and Thomas Schirrmacher. Nashville, TN: B&H, 2008, 558–96.

Mawson, T. J. "The Possibility of a Free-will Defence for the Problem of Natural Evil," *Religious Studies* 40 (2004): 23–42.

Phillips, D. Z. *The Problem of Evil and the Problem of God*. Minneapolis, MN: Fortress Press, 2005.

Root, Jerry. "C. S. Lewis and the Problem of Evil," in *C. S. Lewis: Lightbearer in the Shadowlands*, ed. Angus Menuge. Wheaton, IL: Crossway, 1997, 353–66.

Swinburne, Richard. "The Problem of Evil," in his *The Existence of God*, second edition. New York: Oxford University Press, 2004, 236–72.

Wright, N. T. *Evil and the Justice of God*. Downers Grove, IL: InverVarsity, 2006.

Zacharias, Ravi. "Is God the Source of My Suffering?" in his *Jesus Among Other Gods*. Nashville, TN: Thomas Nelson, 2002, 103–39.

7

CHRISTIANITY'S CULTURAL LEGACY

POISON OR PANACEA?

Korey D. Maas

INTRODUCTION

For obvious reasons, the defense of the faith offered by Christian apologists has typically been precisely that, a defense of the *faith*, that is, a defense of those truth claims of which the Christian faith consists. Yet it is equally obvious that Christianity's critics have never limited their hostility solely to its truth claims, but have directed it also at what they perceive to be its ill effects and baneful consequences. Indeed, this line of attack seems in some respects to have become the most prominent in recent years, with the charge that Christianity is false often being eclipsed by the accusation that it is evil.

Those most prominently amplifying this accusation are well known as the "new atheists," though both the tone and content of their charges reveal just how little is new about the accusation itself. When Steven Weinberg confidently suggests that anything which can be done "to weaken the hold of religion should be done, and may in fact be our greatest contribution to civilization,"[1] he merely echoes the thesis of the nineteenth-century freethinker Charles Bradlaugh (1833–1891), who argued that "the gradual and growing rejection of Christianity . . . has, in fact, added, and will add, to man's happiness and well-being."[2] When Richard Dawkins describes religion as "a significant force for evil in the world,"[3] if not quite the "root of all evil,"[4] he simply summarizes Thomas Paine's more colorfully worded eighteenth-century charge that "the most detestable wickedness, the most horrid cruelties, and the greatest miseries that have afflicted the

---

[1] George Johnson, "A Free-for-All on Science and Religion," *New York Times*, 21 November 2006, F1.

[2] Charles Bradlaugh, "Humanity's Gain from Unbelief," in *Atheism: A Reader*, ed. S. T. Joshi (Amherst: Prometheus, 2000), 171–72.

[3] Richard Dawkins, *The God Delusion* (Boston: Mariner, 2008), 297.

[4] *Root of All Evil?* is the title of the 2006 documentary written and presented by Dawkins; he has since remarked that he disliked the title, which was not his own invention. See *The God Delusion*, 23.

human race have had their origin in this thing called revelation, or revealed religion."[5] Even more telling, Dawkins' portrayal of the Christian church's most visible representative as "an enemy of humanity," and Christianity itself as a "vile, depraved, inhuman theory,"[6] hardly differs from the common accusations of ancient Romans such as Tacitus, who judged Christianity a "pernicious superstition" guilty of various "abominations" and a general "hatred of the human race."[7]

Among the new atheists, however, such charges are most potently distilled in the polemic of the late Christopher Hitchens, who even insists that he is "not so much an atheist as an *anti*-theist,"[8] and so charges Christianity not only with being a fairy-tale, but "a sinister fairy-tale."[9] Hitchens' vigorous anti-theism is most fully on display in his bestselling *God is Not Great: How Religion Poisons Everything*, the subtitle of which nearly says it all. Lest one miss the not-so-subtle point, however, he includes within clarifying chapter titles such as "Is Religion Child Abuse?" and "Religion Kills," and goes on to explain that organized religion is "violent, irrational, intolerant, allied to racism and tribalism and bigotry, invested in ignorance and hostile to free inquiry, contemptuous of women and coercive toward children."[10] Moreover, "it has subsisted largely on lies and fears, and

---

[5] Thomas Paine, *The Age of Reason* (New York: Simon & Schuster, 1976), 182.

[6] These remarks were made in an 18 September 2010 speech in London, protesting Pope Benedict XVI's visit to England. The text of the speech, titled "Ratzinger is an Enemy of Humanity," is available at http://richarddawkins.net/articles/521113-ratzinger-is-an-enemy-of-humanity (accessed 26 October 2010).

[7] Tacitus, *Annals*, 15.44.

[8] Christopher Hitchens and Douglas Wilson, *Is Christianity Good for the World? A Debate* (Moscow, ID: Canon Press, 2008), 12; emphasis in original.

[9] Hitchens and Wilson, *Is Christianity Good for the World*, 14.

[10] From *God is Not Great: How Religion Poisons Everything* by Christopher Hitchens (New York: Twelve, 2007), 56. Copyright © 2007 by

been the accomplice of ignorance and guilt as well as of slavery, genocide, racism, and tyranny."[11] In other words, "religion is not just amoral, but positively immoral";[12] indeed, as he insists in another work, "[i]t cannot be said often enough that this preachment is immoral."[13]

Upon being confronted with such charges, it is perhaps only natural that the Christian feel compelled to rebut them. It will be prudent to acknowledge from the outset, though, that, given a choice, this is not the particular "fight" the Christian apologist will be most eager to pick—and for a number of reasons. First, as a simple matter of historical record, it will be impossible to deny that the institutional church and her members have often been implicated in the sorts of evils for which Hitchens and others condemn them. More importantly, even if it could be demonstrated that all Christians everywhere and at all times have been blameless paragons of virtue, the apologist's goal is never simply to defend Christians, but to defend Christianity. Even hypothetically model Christian behavior, however, would in no way substantiate the veracity of Christian belief, as Hitchens himself is keen to point out: "virtuous behavior by a believer is no proof at all of—indeed it is not even an argument for—the truth of his belief."[14] Equally worth noting in this context, though, is the converse. Therefore, in engaging this line of contention one will want consistently to emphasize that even if it could be documented that none were so wicked as Christians, this would not be

---

[11] Hitchens, *God is Not Great*, 229. By permission of Grand Central Publishing. All rights reserved.

[12] Hitchens, *God is Not Great*, 205. By permission of Grand Central Publishing. All rights reserved.

[13] Christopher Hitchens, ed., *The Portable Atheist: Essential Readings for the Nonbeliever* (Philadelphia: De Capo, 2007), xvi.

[14] Hitchens, *God is Not Great*, 184–85. By permission of Grand Central Publishing. All rights reserved.

proof of—indeed, not even an argument for—the falsity of Christian theological claims.

Nevertheless, to the extent that such charges concerning Christian behavior might dissuade people from giving any serious hearing to Christian proclamation, they will be worth addressing. Limitations of space preclude detailed treatment of each specific accusation leveled by even one of Christianity's contemporary critics; but, as the foregoing makes clear, these typically reduce to the general accusation of "evil" or "immorality," most specifically as it involves harm to others. In entering a defense it will be important to note that, by appealing especially to the evidence of past evils such as slavery, the arguments of Hitchens and his colleagues take on a fundamentally historical nature. Before addressing what can only be described as an astonishingly inadequate (if not intentionally distorted) understanding of history, however, even more fundamental—and arguably irresolvable—philosophical problems in Hitchens' polemic deserve attention.

PROBLEMATIC PRELIMINARIES

The single most pressing question in light of the repeated accusations of Christianity's profound evil is, quite simply, whether there is any basis on which objective categories of good and evil might be grounded. Being an anti-theist, Hitchens cannot of course ground the reality of moral categories in the nature, will, or word of any transcendent deity; and indeed, he asserts that "morality requires no supernatural sanction."[15] Having rejected any belief in the supernatural, however, Hitchens leaves himself recourse only to the natural. The physical and chemical laws governing natural

---

[15] Hitchens and Wilson, *Is Christianity Good for the World*, 23. Compare, though, even prominent atheist philosopher J. L. Mackie, who has famously admitted: "Moral properties constitute so odd a cluster of properties and relations that they are most unlikely to have arisen in the ordinary course of events without an all-powerful god to create them." J. L. Mackie, *The Miracle of Theism* (Oxford: Clarendon, 1982), 115; used by permission of Oxford University Press.

phenomena can hardly be equated with moral laws meant to govern human behavior, however, and so Hitchens is at least consistent in speaking of "an indifferent cosmos," calling it "the overwhelmingly probable state of the case."[16]

He is less consistent, though, in failing to push the implications of this conviction to their logical conclusion, as even fellow atheist Richard Dawkins does when he describes an indifferent universe as necessarily having, "at the bottom, no design, no purpose, *no evil and no good*, nothing but pitiless indifference."[17] Believing this to be precisely the case, consistent philosophical naturalists such as E. O. Wilson and Michael Ruse logically conclude that, "[c]onsidered as a rationally justifiable set of claims about an objective something, ethics is illusory."[18] Compared to the "new" atheists, an "old" atheist such as Nietzsche could state the case even more bluntly: on atheism's naturalistic presuppositions, he insisted, "[t]here are altogether no moral facts."[19] Such a logically necessary conclusion ill serves Hitchens' desire to fulminate against the "evils" of Christianity, however, and so he is forced simply to assert the reality of good and evil despite a complete inability to justify this belief.[20] The obvious irony to be noted here is that the new atheist program

---

[16] Hitchens and Wilson, *Is Christianity Good for the World*, 32.

[17] Richard Dawkins, "God's Utility Function," *Scientific American* (November 1995), 85; emphasis added.

[18] Michael Ruse, "Evolutionary Theory and Christian Ethics," in *The Darwinian Paradigm*, ed. Michael Ruse (London: Routledge, 1989), 262. See also Michael Ruse and E. O. Wilson, "The Evolution of Ethics," in *Philosophy of Biology*, ed. Michael Ruse (New York: Macmillan, 1989), 316.

[19] Friedrich Nietzsche, *Twilight of the Idols and The Anti-Christ* (New York: Penguin, 1968), 55. On the same page he further remarks, "Moral judgments agree with religious ones in believing in realities which are no realities."

[20] For Douglas Wilson's repeatedly ignored attempts to elicit some justification, see Hitchens and Wilson, *Is Christianity Good for the World*, 34, 40, 41, 48, and 64.

consists of nothing if not the concerted effort to disabuse people of unjustified beliefs.

Nevertheless, Hitchens' tirades against alleged Christian evils are even more confused. A rationally justifiable charge of immorality must proceed not only on a warranted belief that real moral laws in fact exist, but also on a warranted belief that those who violate such laws may be held culpable. Hitchens certainly believes they are; as Douglas Wilson notes in dialogue with him, "[i]n your choice of words, the people you denounce are to be *blamed*."[21] Yet to lay blame for actions beyond all control would be absurd, and so inhering in the concept of culpability is some notion of free will. To be sure, Hitchens wants to believe that humans are possessed of free will; indeed, he partially predicates his anti-theism on the belief that God's existence "would mean that words like 'freedom' or terms like 'free will' were devoid of all meaning."[22] As with his desire to embrace the factual reality of moral norms, however, it is rather his own commitment to philosophical naturalism which, logically followed, renders the notion of free will meaningless. However much death, destruction, and misery might result from natural phenomena such as tsunamis or earthquakes, these do not freely choose to wreak havoc and cannot choose to do so, and so rational individuals do not hotly denounce them with morally freighted vocabulary. But if even human actions, on naturalistic grounds, must be reduced to natural phenomena unfolding as blind chance and necessity operate upon matter and energy, there can be no rational justification for positing the existence of free will. Again, Hitchens appears blissfully—even willfully—ignorant of that which more logically consistent naturalists recognize: "our conception of reality simply does not allow for radical freedom."[23] Thus, just as objective moral categories must be

---

[21] Hitchens and Wilson, *Is Christianity Good for the World*, 64; emphasis in original.

[22] Hitchens and Wilson, *Is Christianity Good for the World*, 12.

[23] Reprinted by permission of the publisher from *Minds, Brains and Science* by John Searle, p. 98, Cambridge, Mass.: Harvard University Press, Copyright © 1984 by John R. Searle.

deemed by the naturalist "illusory," so too can he or she only speak, as Dawkins does, of the "illusion of free will."[24]

In summary, any denunciation of Christianity predicated upon its being culpable for actions which are in fact evil must proceed from a belief in real moral laws which might or might not be followed by agents possessed of free will. Yet these beliefs simply cannot rationally be warranted in light of the philosophical naturalism embraced by Hitchens himself. His entire project is therefore undermined and collapses upon itself from the start.

The above however, are hardly the sum of Hitchens' logical difficulties. For one whose entire case against religion is essentially predicated upon the conviction that it causes evil effects, his treatment of cause and effect is consistently marred by the *cum hoc* fallacy; that is, wherever he finds religion even remotely associated with some atrocity, he assumes and then asserts it as the primary cause. This is often the case even when such a conclusion approaches absurdity, as, for example, when attempting to implicate Christianity even in the crimes of Joseph Stalin's atheistic absolutism by noting that Stalin had once attended seminary.[25] Moreover, such rhetorical sleights of hand are made despite Hitchens' occasionally veering toward a recognition that the culprit is often not religion *per se*, but its political abuse by cynical and often non-religious rulers. This was precisely the point of Edward Gibbon's famous observation—quoted, but apparently misunderstood, by Hitchens—that the various religions of ancient Rome, though widely disbelieved, were considered "by the magistrate as equally useful."[26]

This reference to various religions highlights another significant problem with the form of Hitchens' arguments. Though the Christian

---

[24] Preston Jones, ed., *Is Belief in God Good, Bad or Irrelevant?* (Downers Grove, IL: InterVarsity, 2006), 91.

[25] Cf. Hitchens and Wilson, *Is Christianity Good for the World*, 37, and Hitchens, *God is Not Great*, 244.

[26] Hitchens, *God is Not Great*, 155. By permission of Grand Central Publishing. All rights reserved.

apologist will be particularly concerned with a defense of Christianity against false accusations, even the title of Hitchens' most popular book makes evident that his own charges are not leveled solely at Christianity; he aims to indict "religion" more generally. Only the fallacy of hasty induction, though, allows one to portray "religion"— whether Amish or jihadist, whether that of Mother Teresa or Khalid Sheikh Mohammed—as equally and inescapably evil in its effects.[27] Thus, even Hitchens' more sober-minded colleagues recognize the illogical nature of such uncritical generalizing; prominent Muslim-cum-atheist Ayaan Hirsi Ali, for example, is more than willing to admit that her own experiences have sufficiently convinced her that not all religions are equally worthy of disdain.[28]

Even more egregious than his hasty generalizations about ill-defined "religion," however, is the equivocation fallacy evident in Hitchens' arbitrary redefinitions of religion to suit his own agenda. Thus, a Bible-quoting Baptist preacher such as Martin Luther King, Jr., is hastily dismissed as being a Christian "in no real as opposed to nominal sense"; instead, says Hitchens, he was merely a "profound humanist."[29] And conversely, the communist totalitarianism of the former Soviet Union should not primarily be understood—as it understood itself—as ideologically atheistic, but as "faith-based"—as allegedly evidenced by its secular analogues to martyrs, saints, icons, and relics.[30]

---

[27] Hitchens does attempt to establish some moral equivalency, though, in his book-length attack on Mother Teresa. See *The Missionary Position: Mother Teresa in Theory and Practice* (New York: Verso, 1995).

[28] Ayaan Hirsi Ali, *Nomad: From Islam to America, a Personal Journey through the Clash of Civilizations* (New York: Free Press, 2010), 212.

[29] Hitchens, *God is Not Great*, 176, 180. By permission of Grand Central Publishing. All rights reserved.

[30] Hitchens, *God is Not Great*, 250; cf. 245–46.

CHRISTIANITY AND SLAVERY: A CASE STUDY

In light of the fundamentally flawed premises and amateurish logical fallacies with which Hitchens' works are shot through, it is perhaps difficult to understand their popularity. Whatever Hitchens' own intentions, though, the strength of his anti-theistic polemic has never been its logical rigor; it has instead been the unreflective emotional responses elicited by his vivid historical anecdotes. Even a brief analysis of his use of history, though, reveals that it is no less deeply flawed than his philosophy. As David Bentley Hart rightly points out, the new atheists as a whole consistently engage in "the kind of historical oversimplifications that are either demonstrably false or irrelevantly true,"[31] and Hitchens' work especially is "so extraordinarily crowded with errors that one soon gives up counting them."[32]

This is especially evident in recurring discussions of Christianity's implication in the institution of slavery, which, as a case study, concisely encapsulate and epitomize the characterization of Christianity as immoral and inhuman. Though not quite so naïve as to repeat Charles Bradlaugh's grossly inaccurate assertion that, "[f]or some 1,800 years almost all Christians kept slaves, bought slaves, sold slaves, bred slaves, stole slaves,"[33] Hitchens comes close when he asserts that "[t]his huge and terrible industry was blessed by *all* churches and for a long time aroused *absolutely no* religious protest."[34] This caricature of Christianity as inherently supportive of slavery is rhetorically effective because slavery, especially in its New World manifestation, was indeed grossly inhuman, and was by no means universally denounced by the Christian churches. But it is especially effective because it flatters modern audiences with illusions of moral superiority allegedly resulting from the progress of

---

[31] David B. Hart, "Believe It or Not," *First Things* (May 2010), 37.

[32] Hart, "Believe It or Not," 38, where numerous examples are provided.

[33] Bradlaugh, "Humanity's Gain from Unbelief," 175.

[34] Hitchens, *God is Not Great*, 176; emphasis added. By permission of Grand Central Publishing. All rights reserved.

enlightened secularism. Illustrative of this is Sam Harris' noting that "[t]he entire civilized world now agrees that slavery is an abomination";[35] and yet its abolition "had to be spread at the point of a bayonet throughout the Confederate South, among the most pious Christians this country has ever known."[36] This is meant to be especially damning because, Harris also insists, "[i]t is remarkably easy for a person to arrive at this epiphany" that "slaves are human beings like himself";[37] the only thing possibly accounting for this epiphany's prevention, therefore, must be the ignorance and malice engendered by Christian theology. This is precisely Hitchens' own point when he asserts, with reference to antebellum America (and without reference to any evidence), "[t]he chance that someone's *secular* or freethinking opinion would cause him or her to denounce the whole injustice was extremely high," while, conversely, "the chance that someone's religious belief would cause him or her to uphold slavery and racism was statistically extremely *high*."[38]

This line of argument, though specifically addressing only the issue of slavery, concisely epitomizes the manner in which the new atheists most typically associate Christianity with the historical sanction of moral evils. In doing so, however, it also epitomizes the egregious disregard of historical fact and the manifold abuses of historical interpretation so typical of popular atheist polemic. Most obviously, the first inconvenient fact which must be ignored if one is to posit a uniquely intimate relationship between Christianity and slavery is that the latter long predates the former. More significantly still, slavery not only existed before Christianity, but it existed almost universally; that is; virtually all societies of pre-Christian antiquity practiced slavery. This was the case even in the most advanced societies, not least the enlightened Greco-Roman culture into which

---

[35] Sam Harris, *Letter to a Christian Nation* (New York: Vintage, 2008), 14.

[36] Harris, *Letter*, 19.

[37] Harris, *Letter*, 19, 18.

[38] Hitchens, *God is Not Great*, 180; emphases in original. By permission of Grand Central Publishing. All rights reserved.

Christianity was born.[39] Indeed, it was the writings of Greece's esteemed philosophers which gave slavery its most prominent and influential sanction. It was, for example, the pre-Christian Aristotle (384–322) who, most influentially for the western world, sanctioned the institution with his theory that some people are by birth and constitution "natural slaves"; they are therefore not to have equal rights with others but are to be deemed no more than "living tools."[40]

It is certainly true that the earliest Christians, a tiny minority in the Roman empire, did not consider the abolition of slavery their most pressing concern. It is also true, as critics ceaselessly observe, that the Christian Scriptures nowhere unambiguously condemn slavery as a moral evil. It deserves emphasizing, though, that the atheists' gleeful emphasis of these points betrays an astonishing hypocrisy in light of their own consistent denunciation of contemporary Christians who might attempt to influence social norms or legal policies—concerning abortion, for example, or same-sex marriage—on account of their faith.

Moreover, this logical inconsistency is once again coupled with a careless disregard for certain historical facts. Though true that Scripture nowhere explicitly denounces slavery, it does quite explicitly establish certain theological propositions which made possible a principled critique of slavery such as had not previously been heard. When what began as a minority sect eventually gained a political voice, these principles were also increasingly called forth in building a case against the slave society in which Christians found themselves. Though certainly continuing to be influenced by this society, and so never unanimously denouncing slavery, the principled objection to it was being voiced even before the legalization of Christianity by Cyprian of Carthage (d. 258), who criticized his contemporary Demetrianus for holding slaves, despite sharing with

---

[39] Indeed, enlightened Greece and Rome are what M. I. Finley, *Ancient Slavery and Modern Ideology* (New York: Viking, 1980), 67, concludes were the first comprehensive slave societies.

[40] See, e.g., Aristotle, *The Politics*, 1.4–5, and *Nicomachean Ethics*, 8.11.

them a common human nature and therefore equal human rights.[41] This appeal to equal rights based in a common human nature is also taken up by the most influential theologian of the church's first five hundred years. Augustine of Hippo (354–430) insisted that God "did not intend that his rational creature, who was made in his own image, should have dominion over anything but the irrational creature—not man over man, but man over beasts." Therefore, again contrary to Aristotle, he can conclude that slavery was "introduced by sin and not by nature," and should thus be recognized as an "inconceivable horror."[42] Even more explicitly, in what is often described as antiquity's most vigorous denunciation of slavery, Gregory of Nyssa (c. 335–394) asks, "If you are equal in all these ways, therefore, in what respect have you something extra, tell me, that you who are human think yourself the master of a human being[?]" To do so, Gregory insists, is to "legislate in competition with God, overturning his law for the human species."[43]

Nor was this merely armchair theorizing or pious postulating; though powerless (and, yes, sometimes unwilling) to effect immediate changes in long established custom, the earliest churches often evidenced their own commitment to equality by recognizing—long before the State did—the legitimacy of slave marriages, freeing their own slaves, and buying freedom for others.[44] Indeed, already at the turn of the first century the author of the *Shepherd of Hermas* is exhorting fellow Christians to redeem slaves with their own money, arguing that one who does not "commits a great sin."[45] More revealingly, even before the close of the first century Clement of

---

[41] Cyprian, *Address to Demetrianus*, cap. 8.

[42] Augustine, *City of God*, 19.15, 19.8.

[43] Gregory of Nyssa, "Fourth Homily on Ecclesiastes," in *Gregory of Nyssa: Homilies on Ecclesiastes*, ed. Stuart George Hall (New York: De Gruyter, 1993), 75, 73.

[44] Henry Chadwick, *The Early Church* (New York: Penguin, 1967), 60.

[45] *Shepherd of Hermas*, Book 3, Parable 1, and Parable 10, cap. 4.

Rome can comment on the number of Christians who have sold themselves into slavery in order to fund the emancipation of others.[46]

If, as the new atheists like to assume, it is "remarkably easy" to recognize the immoral nature of slavery, one is forced to ask why, among the ubiquitous slave societies of antiquity, "only in Christianity did the idea develop that slavery was sinful and must be abolished?"[47] Given their agenda, as well as their audience, however, Hitchens and his colleagues often find it preferable to ignore the issue of slavery in antiquity—and its decline under Christian influence—and to focus instead on its later reemergence in the New World. This allows them to raise the very different, but equally pointed question: if Christianity is alleged to be fundamentally antithetical to slavery, what accounts for its reestablishment and defense in the New World—which was colonized by professing Christians?

Though meant to be strictly rhetorical, this is a better question than its posers appear to realize. Better still, though, is the following formulation: what accounts for the reinstitution of slavery in the New World colonized by Christians—especially since this was from the start vigorously opposed by the church's spokesmen, from its local missionaries, up through its supervising bishops, all the way to the pope himself? There is, of course, no denying that the New World reestablishment of slavery—first of the indigenous population, later of Africans—was carried out by those who claimed affiliation with the Christian church. But contrary to Hitchens' claims that this was "blessed by *all* churches and for a long time aroused *absolutely no* religious protest," it was, in the earliest era of colonization by Europe's Catholic powers, precisely those vested with authority in the church who condemned this development as antithetical to Christianity. Especially revealing is that the institution's most vocal detractors were often of the Dominican order, those most prominently tasked throughout the late medieval and early modern eras with

---

[46] Clement of Rome, *First Epistle to the Corinthians*, cap. 55.

[47] Rodney Stark, *For the Glory of God: How Monotheism Led to Reformations, Science, Witch-Hunts, and the End of Slavery* (Princeton: Princeton University Press, 2003), 291.

defining and defending Catholic orthodoxy. How far slavery was judged to be compatible with orthodox belief is evident in the common Dominican practice—inaugurated by Antonio de Montesinos (d. 1545), one of the first missionaries to arrive in the New World—of denying confession and absolution to those owning slaves.[48] Even more pointedly, though, this incompatibility was made evident in a continual series of papal bulls, unambiguously condemning slavery, and threatening excommunication for its practice, dating from the very beginning of Spanish colonization in the fifteenth century.[49]

The question therefore remains: in light of such clear opposition from the church, how did the earliest and ostensibly Christian conquistadors and colonists justify slavery? In large part, just as their classical pagan forebears had: by appeal to Aristotle.[50] Nowhere was this made more explicit than in the formal debate convened in 1550 at Valladolid, Spain, by the Emperor Charles V, with the intent of clarifying the Spanish position on New World slavery. Defending the practice was Juan Gines de Sepulveda (1489–1573), an esteemed jurist who had only recently published his own translation of Aristotle's *Politics*, the work in which his doctrine of "natural slavery" was most comprehensively detailed.[51] So evident did

---

[48] See Gustavo Gutiérrez, *Las Casas*, tr. Robert R. Barr (Maryknoll: Orbis, 1993), 33.

[49] See Joel Panzer, *The Popes and Slavery* (New York: Alba House, 1996), 19–22.

[50] See Lewis Hanke, *Aristotle and the American Indians: A Study in Race Prejudice in the Modern World* (Bloomington, IN: Indiana University Press, 1959).

[51] In an attempt to justify enslavement of New World natives, Sepulveda had also recently composed *The Second Democrates, or, The Just Causes of the War against the Indians*. Especially worth noting with reference to this work and its argument is that the panel of theologians who examined it at the Crown's request judged it doctrinally unsound, recommending that it be denied the royal license necessary for publication. See Anthony Pagden, "Introduction," in Bartolomé de las Casas, *A Short Account of the Destruction of the Indies* (New York: Penguin, 1992), xxviii–xxix.

Sepulveda make it that the defense of slavery rested not on the authority of Christian Scripture, but of the pagan Aristotle, that his opponent, the influential Dominican theologian Bartolomé de las Casas (c. 1484–1566), was compelled to conclude their debate on this point with a curt, "Good-bye, Aristotle!"[52]

The authority of Aristotle to sanction the institution of slavery was severely dented, not only by critiques of Las Casas and others concerned with slavery, but also on account of Aristotle's more thorough displacement by the natural philosophy arising with the Enlightenment. Yet neither Aristotle's fall nor the Enlightenment's rise curtailed the growth and defense of slavery in the West. Indeed, as even the secularist philosopher Jesse Prinz is willing to acknowledge, "slavery became more prevalent *after* the Enlightenment."[53] This must only perplex those embracing the popular narrative of a secular Enlightenment banishing Christendom's cruel prejudices and ushering in an age of liberty, equality, and fraternity.

But slavery's advance in tandem with the Enlightenment is hardly accidental. Though displacing Aristotle, the most prominent philosophers of the Enlightenment merely replaced his defense of slavery with an even more forceful, allegedly more "scientific," justification for the practice. Thus, not only would such giants of the Enlightenment as Voltaire (1694–1778), Thomas Hobbes (1588–1679), and John Locke (1632–1704) refuse to support the cause of abolition, they vigorously championed the institution of slavery itself, the latter even investing in the Atlantic slave trade.[54] Most significantly, however, as indigenous slaves were replaced by Africans, the institution was increasingly and explicitly justified by the Enlightenment's novel theories of race. The French *philosophes*,

---

[52] Bartolomé de las Casas, *In Defense of the Indians*, tr. Stafford Poole (DeKalb, IL: Northern Illinois University Press, 1992), 40.

[53] Jesse Prinz, "Morality is a Culturally Conditioned Response," *Philosophy Now* (January/February 2011), 7; emphasis in original.

[54] K. G. Davies, *The Royal African Company* (New York: Atheneum, 1970), 58 n. 5, 62–65.

for example, in compiling their seminal *Encyclopédie*, would include under the entry for "Nègre" the judgment that he would "appear to constitute a new species."[55] Voltaire, perhaps the era's most caustic critic of Christianity, located this "new species" in a hierarchy just above "apes and oysters."[56] David Hume (1711–1776), beloved by modern skeptics for allegedly discrediting any record of the miraculous, could also offer that the black race was "naturally inferior to the whites."[57] Similarly, Immanuel Kant (1724–1804), though primarily remembered and often revered for his philosophical attack on the traditional proofs for God's existence, in fact devoted more university lectures to race than to any other topic. His conclusion: "Humanity is at its greatest perfection in the race of whites."[58] It would of course be inaccurate to claim that all Enlightenment skeptics embraced such theories, or that none opposed slavery; and yet, as Jewish commentator David Brog rightly observes, "none embraced the abolition of slavery as their mission in life the way so many Christian activists of that era did."[59] It is therefore not surprising that an opponent of abolition such as England's Lord Melbourne (d. 1853) could criticize it on precisely these grounds: "Things have come to a

---

[55] Emmanuel Chukwudi Eze, ed., *Race and the Enlightenment: A Reader* (Malden, MA: Blackwell, 1997), 91.

[56] Robert Bernasconi, "Who Invented the Concept of Race? Kant's Role in the Enlightenment Construction of Race," in *Race*, ed. Robert Bernasconi (Malden, MA: Blackwell, 2001), 21.

[57] David Hume, "Of National Characters," in *David Hume: Essays Moral, Political, and Literary*, ed. Eugene F. Miller (Indianapolis: Liberty Fund, 1987), 208 n. 10.

[58] Eze, *Race and the Enlightenment*, 63. See also David Brion Davis, *Slavery and Human Progress* (New York: Oxford University Press, 1984), 131, for note of the regular critique of such racial theories by Christian abolitionists, who recognized them as an un-Christian Enlightenment invention.

[59] David Brog, *In Defense of Faith: The Judeo-Christian Idea and the Struggle for Humanity* (New York: Encounter, 2010), 305.

pretty pass," he remarked, "when one should permit religion to invade public life."[60]

Such a dismissal of concerns about slavery is revealing in two important respects. It not only conveys accurately the fact that the movement to abolish the institution was an overwhelmingly "religious" movement, but it also reveals that slavery's proponents were well aware of this. Indeed, however difficult this fact might be for modern critics such as Hitchens and Harris to recognize, it was nearly impossible for those of the time to be ignorant of it. Melbourne himself would have been well aware that the organized antislavery movement in his own country began among the Quakers—who had expelled slaveholders from membership already in 1777 and who would comprise three-fourths of the committee founding the Society for the Abolition of the Slave Trade in the following year[61]—and that subsequently, "[r]eligion was the central concern of all the British abolitionist leaders."[62] Nor were the concerns on this side of the Atlantic noticeably different; not only were those states populated primarily by Quakers and Puritans the first to reform and abolish existing slave laws,[63] but by 1835 fully two-thirds of active abolitionists were Christian clergy.[64] Thus the American historian Gilbert Barnes could describe the antislavery movement here in precisely the same terms as Britain's: "From the beginning the

---

[60] Eric Metaxas, *Amazing Grace: William Wilberforce and the Heroic Campaign to End Slavery* (New York: HarperOne, 2007), xix.

[61] Michael Craton, James Walvin, and David Wright, *Slavery, Abolition and Emancipation: Black Slaves and the British Empire* (New York: Longman, 1976), 195.

[62] Davis, *Slavery and Human Progress*, 139.

[63] See Arthur Zilversmit, *The First Emancipation: The Abolition of Slavery in the North* (Chicago: Chicago University Press, 1967), 85–109.

[64] Sherwood E. Wirt, *The Social Consequences of the Evangelical* (New York: Harper & Row, 1968), 39. Of the local agents of the American Anti-Slavery Society during the same decade, John Auping, *Religion and Social Justice: The Case of Christianity and the Abolition of Slavery in America* (Mexico City: Universidad Iberoamericana, 1994), 103, finds that fully 75% were clergy.

movement had been inextricably bound up with the churches. The churches were its forums and the houses of its local organization; from the churches it drew its justifying inspiration."[65]

Just as it has been acknowledged that supporters of a secularizing Enlightenment did not uniformly defend slavery, it cannot be denied that many American Christians did defend the practice, and often did so as having explicit biblical sanction. Yet it is worth recalling Gibbon's observation about appeals to religion often being masks for self-interest. It is hardly surprising that those invested in the institution of slavery might appeal to an authority they recognized as holding sway with the great majority of their fellow citizens. Among truly disinterested Christians, though, such as those living outside of the United States, "there was only contempt for efforts to defend slavery on the basis of the Bible."[66]

No less significant is something like the converse; that is, a great deal of contempt was also shown by slavery's supporters for the abolitionist movement's clear and consistent association with Christianity. Typical in this regard is not only Lord Melbourne's previously noted comment, but similarly, in America, Maryland Congressman Michael J. Stone's (1747–1812) remark that abolitionism was being fueled by the "disposition of religious sects to imagine that they understood the rights of human nature better than all the world besides."[67] Here again the disjunction between the facile revisionism of the new atheists and the firm convictions of their predecessors becomes obvious. Whereas Sam Harris can, with the benefit of two centuries' hindsight, opine on how "remarkably easy" it is to recognize the moral horror of slavery, its eighteenth-century

---

[65] Gilbert H. Barnes, *The Anti-Slavery Impulse* (New York: Harbinger, 1964), 98.

[66] Mark Noll, *America's God: From Jonathan Edwards to Abraham Lincoln* (New York: Oxford University Press, 2002), 400; used by permission of Oxford University Press, USA.

[67] W. E. B. Du Bois, *The Suppression of the African Slave-Trade to the United States of America, 1638–1870* (New York: Longmans, Green, and Co., 1904), 75.

supporters testify that, among "all the world," it was almost exclusively within the denominations of Christianity that this conclusion was reached.

CHRISTIANITY, CULTURE, AND (BORROWED) CAPITAL

It is worth noting again that the particular issue of slavery is here addressed not only because it is frequently raised in anti-theistic polemic, but also because it is, in important respects, representative of the whole panoply of oppressive evils supposed to spring organically from Christianity. Slavery shares in common with Hitchens' similar charges of genocide, racism, and sexism the fundamental mistake which Harris deems so easy to avoid: the failure to recognize that others "are human beings like [one]self." Put another way, such evils result from a failure to grasp what the American founders believed not only easily discernible, but even "self-evident"—that "all men are created equal." As lamentable as this ignorance has been, it should not be entirely shocking, for the simple fact is that the innate equality of all human beings is not rationally self-evident. Indeed, as Vincent Carroll and David Shiflett remark, the *Declaration of Independence*'s claim to the contrary could be made and read without the temptation to "laugh out loud" only because it was the product of a culture steeped in the Christian heritage.[68] The unchallenged ubiquity of slavery in pre-Christian antiquity is merely one prominent example illustrative of this point, and so David Bentley Hart speaks without exaggeration when he notes that any assertion of human equality made in the pre-Christian world would have been found "not so much foolish as unintelligible."[69] The significant implications of this point can hardly be overstated, not least because they bear not only on how

---

[68] Vincent Carroll and David Shiflett, *Christianity on Trial: Arguments Against Anti-Religious Bigotry* (San Francisco: Encounter, 2002), 3.

[69] David Bentley Hart, *Atheist Delusions: The Christian Revolution and Its Fashionable Enemies* (New Haven: Yale University Press, 2009), 32–33.

one interprets Christianity's influence upon the past, but also on how one envisions a future with—or without—Christian influence.

Those who dissent from a vision such as Charles Bradlaugh's, with its assumption of utopia unfolding in proportion to Christianity declining, often point out how naïve Bradlaugh's nineteenth-century view appears in light of the unparalleled twentieth-century atrocities committed in the name of officially atheist (or neo-pagan) regimes. Whatever one makes of this line of critique, it has been voiced often enough that contemporary atheists feel compelled to address it in various ways. Abandoning the staunch commitment to the *cum hoc* fallacy evident throughout his treatment of sins committed by Christians, Dawkins, for example, simply blusters that there is "not the smallest evidence" that atheism might negatively influence morality;[70] like an exasperated schoolmarm he wags his finger at Pope Benedict XVI, asking, "How *dare* Ratzinger suggest that atheism has any connection whatsoever" to the crimes of Stalin or Hitler?[71] As alluded to previously, though, Hitchens himself takes a more subtle, yet more revealing tack. Despite acknowledging the official atheism of Stalin's Russia, for example, he attempts to portray its manifold injustices as arising not from its atheist ideology, but from the lingering influence of its long Orthodox past.[72]

However disingenuous such arguments might be, what is especially revealing here is Hitchens' explicit willingness to recognize something like the concept of "borrowed capital." But such a concept is a double-edged sword, and all evidence indicates that Hitchens wields the blunter edge. Far more convincing than his suggestion that post-Christian societies have remained negatively influenced primarily by their Christian pasts is the thesis that such societies remain committed to the virtues and values most cherished by modern—even secular—civilization largely to the extent that they

---

[70] Dawkins, *The God Delusion*, 309.

[71] Dawkins, "Ratzinger is an Enemy of Humanity"; emphasis in original.

[72] Hitchens and Wilson, *Is Christianity Good for the World*, 37; Hitchens, *God is Not Great*, 244–46.

remain influenced, consciously or unconsciously, by their Christian heritage.[73] The belief that all people—regardless of race, nationality, sex, age, or abilities—are to be considered equally human is, though hugely important, only the most fundamental of such influences. Far more important with respect to the moral concerns raised by Hitchens and others is the question of what ethical significance human equality is supposed to have. One might insist, for example, that all rocks are, on account of their shared rockiness, to be deemed essentially equal; yet this says nothing at all about how rocks should be treated. But the biblical account of humanity's divine creation, out of which western notions of human equality grew, further proclaims that man was created in the image and likeness of God himself, thus providing the foundation upon which the moral concepts of unique human worth and dignity were constructed.

Such a conclusion, it must immediately be emphasized, is not simply special pleading on the part of Christian apologists; it is the very conclusion firmly and consistently voiced even by Christianity's harshest critics. Stephen Pinker, for example, in an essay unblushingly titled "The Stupidity of Dignity," complains that the concept is "fed by fervent religious impulses," most specifically the "quite extraordinary" teachings of the Christian Scriptures.[74] Naturalist philosophers Helga Kuhse and Peter Singer likewise dismiss the concept because they recognize that the only possible way to justify beliefs in human equality or dignity would be to ground them in something like the biblical account of creation.[75] Singer

---

[73] Bruce Sheiman, himself an atheist, rightly notes: "We must not forget that whatever ethical culture prevails today in our secular society was formed over centuries of religious moral education as an antecedent." Bruce Sheiman, *An Atheist Defends Religion: Why Humanity is Better Off with Religion than Without It* (New York: Alpha, 2009), 39. Similarly, Hart remarks, "A post-Christian unbeliever is still, most definitely, for good or for ill, post-*Christian*." Hart, *Atheist Delusions*, 108; emphasis in original.

[74] Steven Pinker, "The Stupidity of Dignity," *The New Republic* (28 May 2008), 29.

[75] Helga Kuhse and Peter Singer, *Should the Baby Live?* (Oxford: Oxford University Press, 1985), 118–39.

himself, perhaps best known for his vocal advocacy of infanticide, is even more direct, insisting that respect for infant life is merely "a distinctively Christian attitude rather than a universal ethical value."[76]

Recognizing that such blunt assessments, and implicit rejections, of the notions of equality and dignity are unlikely to find favor even among modern secularists—however logical they may be on a secularist worldview—some are quick to assert that renouncing God "does not compel us to renounce the moral, cultural and spiritual values that have been formulated in his name."[77] This may indeed be the case, and yet it begs the question: how are such "values" to be justified once divorced from the doctrine which originally gave them warrant? Why should they be deemed morally binding in any objective sense? It is quite evident, for example, that such values are not even remotely universal. Not only were they judged absurd among even the most enlightened pre-Christian cultures; they are increasingly rejected in our own post-Christian context. Thus Singer speaks almost prophetically when he asserts that, "Once the religious mumbo jumbo surrounding the term 'human' has been stripped away ... we will not regard as sacrosanct the life of each and every member of our species."[78] Thus the ostensibly ethically minded founder of People for the Ethical Treatment of Animals can similarly confess, "I don't believe that human beings have 'the right to life,' " considering the notion a "perversion."[79]

One need not invoke Hitler's Third Reich to demonstrate that such statements, if taken seriously, readily serve to sanction the very sorts of evils Hitchens finds uniquely religious. Such is evident, to

---

[76] Peter Singer, *Practical Ethics* 3rd edition (New York: Cambridge University Press, 1993), 172. Copyright © 1980, 1993, 2011 Peter Singer. Reprinted with the permission of Cambridge University Press.

[77] Andre Comte-Sponville, *The Little Book of Atheist Spirituality*, tr. Nancy Huston (New York: Penguin, 2008), 21.

[78] Peter Singer, "Sanctity of Life or Quality of Life?" *Pediatrics* 72 (July 1983), 129.

[79] Katie McCabe, "Who Will Live, Who Will Die?" *Washingtonian* 21 (August 1986), 215.

cite only one infamous example, in Supreme Court Justice Oliver Wendell Holmes's (1841–1935) majority opinion in *Buck v. Bell* (1927), legitimizing the forced sterilization of those deemed "unfit" to reproduce. Such action could be placed on the same moral plane as spaying or neutering one's cat because, according to Holmes, there is "no reason for attributing to man a significance different in kind from that which belongs to a baboon or a grain of sand."[80] Indeed, said Holmes, of all the ridiculous ideas one might embrace, the "hyper-aethereal respect for human life seems perhaps the silliest of all."[81]

But if the manner in which human beings are to be treated cannot be informed by a belief in innate dignity and equality—because such notions must logically be jettisoned with the rejection of the theology which justified them—what is to inform, and ultimately ground, human morality? Hitchens' own answer, inevitable in light of his naturalistic presuppositions, is as unambiguous as it is flawed: "Our morality evolved."[82] As detailed above, however, such a view cannot allow even for the prerequisites of serious moral discourse: objective categories of good and evil, and the free will to choose between them. And once again, this is widely acknowledged even by those sharing Hitchens' own convictions. James Rachels, for instance, summarizes the commonly shared view that the neo-Darwinian theory of evolution is a "universal solvent";[83] that is, it erodes not only competing beliefs in a divine creation, but also any assessments of human nature and human morality derived from them. Thus, he concludes, "traditional supports for the idea of human dignity are gone," and so, "a Darwinian may conclude that a successful defense

---

[80] Mary Ann Glendon, "The Bearable Lightness of Dignity," *First Things* (May 2011), 42.

[81] Albert Alschuler, *Law Without Morals* (Chicago: University of Chicago Press, 2000), 26.

[82] Hitchens and Wilson, *Is Christianity Good for the World*, 59.

[83] The notion of Darwinism as a "universal acid" was popularized by Daniel C. Dennett; see, e.g., his *Darwin's Dangerous Idea: Evolution and the Meanings of Life* (New York: Simon & Schuster, 1995), 63.

of human dignity is most unlikely."[84] Illustrating this point most starkly is perhaps the most prominent scientist of our day, Stephen Hawking, whose own commitment to naturalism leads him to conclude emphatically that "the human race is just a chemical scum on a moderate-sized planet."[85] Given such conclusions, Richard Dawkins, the foremost apostle of both neo-Darwinism and the new atheism, can be judged guilty only of understatement when he writes that "[a] good case can be made that a society run on Darwinian lines would be a very disagreeable society in which to live."[86] Indeed, the irony of Hitchens' appeal to a Darwinian morality over against allegedly Christian immorality is compounded on the testimony of Charles Darwin himself; commenting on the influence of Christian missionary activity in the lands to which he traveled, he noted of such historically common evils as human sacrifice, infanticide, and the targeting of even women and children in warfare, that these had been abolished "by the introduction of Christianity." More pointedly, he added, "to forget these things is base ingratitude."[87]

CONCLUSION

By way of introduction it was noted that there is little "new" in the new atheist polemic against Christianity as a fundamentally immoral creed which, as such, has historically sanctioned a plethora of social evils. New atheists such as Hitchens are in perfect agreement with their forebears in the nineteenth century, and even in pagan antiquity, in charging Christianity with inaugurating, in Nietzsche's term, a "transvaluation" of all values. Indeed, much like Hitchens, the self-styled "Antichrist" Nietzsche predicated his entire case against

---

[84] James Rachels, *Created from Animals* (Oxford: Oxford University Press, 1990), 172; used by permission of Oxford University Press.

[85] David Deutsch, *The Fabric of Reality* (New York: Viking, 1997), 177–78.

[86] Richard Dawkins, "The Illusion of Design," *Natural History* (November 2005), 37.

[87] Charles Darwin, *Voyage of the Beagle* (Garden City, NY: Doubleday, 1962), 413.

Christianity on the profound social, cultural, and moral consequences wrought by it. And yet there is a radical disjunction, an introduction of something obviously new, between the "old" atheism of Nietzsche and the new atheism of Hitchens. The very "evils" denounced as uniquely Christian by both Nietzsche and ancient pagans—elevating the status of women, caring for the poor, protecting the young and the disabled—are precisely the sorts of values Hitchens lauds, only denying that Christianity had anything to do with justifying or popularizing them. Nietzsche, though, remains not only the better philosopher, but unquestionably the better historian. And his recognition of the profound moral consequences of Christianity's rise is coupled with a clear-eyed vision of the equally profound consequences which would follow its demise: the related demise of "our whole European morality."[88]

It is again worth reiterating, though, that even a successful defense of Christianity against charges of inherent and systemic immorality does nothing to establish the veracity of its theological truth claims. As such, it is not, and cannot be, a defense of the Christian faith *per se*. The undermining of popular anti-Christian prejudices may, however, serve to break down barriers preventing any thoughtful consideration of Christian claims. Moreover, any extended engagement with the moral argument against Christianity might eventually reveal what is very often the unstated, but in fact fundamental, objection to Christianity and the ethos growing organically out of it. The late Bertrand Russell (1870–1970), Cambridge philosopher and most prominent atheist of the twentieth century, stated this most unguardedly when noting that there is very little one might say against the Christian ethos except that it is exceedingly difficult to fulfill.[89]

Indeed, not only difficult to fulfill, but impossible to fulfill perfectly. Thus, even while defending Christianity's ennobling effects

---

[88] Friedrich Nietzsche, *The Portable Nietzsche*, ed. W. Kaufmann (New York: Penguin, 1982), 447.

[89] Bertrand Russell, *A History of Western Philosophy* (New York: Simon & Schuster, 1972), 579.

on western culture, the apologist will insist that the individuals inhabiting this and all cultures—Christians and non-Christians alike—remain imperfect, immoral, *sinful*; and so in need of the forgiveness of sins. Here, then, the apologist enters the heart of the matter, proclaiming and defending the existence of a God who can and does forgive, the trustworthy Scriptures which testify to this forgiveness, the divine Christ and his atoning death and resurrection which exclusively establish this forgiveness, and the ultimate answer to the question of evil provided by this forgiveness.

FOR FURTHER READING

Brog, David. *In Defense of Faith: The Judeo-Christian Idea and the Struggle for Humanity*. New York: Encounter, 2010.

Carroll, Vincent, and David Shiflett. *Christianity on Trial: Arguments against Anti-Religious Bigotry*. San Francisco: Encounter, 2002.

D'Souza, Dinesh. *What's So Great About Christianity*. Carol Stream, IL: Tyndale House, 2007.

Hart, David Bentley. *Atheist Delusions: The Christian Revolution and Its Fashionable Enemies*. New Haven: Yale University Press, 2009.

Hill, Jonathan. *What Has Christianity Ever Done for Us? How It Shaped the Modern World*. Downers Grove, IL: InterVarsity, 2005.

Hitchens, Christopher, and Douglas Wilson. *Is Christianity Good for the World? A Debate*. Moscow, ID: Canon Press, 2008.

Linville, Mark D. "The Moral Argument," in *The Blackwell Companion to Natural Theology*, ed. William Lane Craig and J. P. Moreland. Oxford: Blackwell, 2009, 391–448.

———. "The Moral Poverty of Evolutionary Naturalism," in *Contending with Christianity's Critics*, ed. Paul Copan and William Lane Craig. Nashville: B&H Academic, 2009, 58–73.

Moreland, J. P. "The Image of God and the Failure of Scientific Atheism," in *God is Great, God is Good: Why Belief in God is Reasonable and Responsible*, ed. William Lane Craig and Chad Meister. Downers Grove, IL: InterVarsity, 2009, 32–48.

Sampson, Philip J. *Six Modern Myths about Christianity and Western Civilization*. Downers Grove, IL: InterVarsity, 2000.

Schmidt, Alvin J. *How Christianity Changed the World*. Grand Rapids: Zondervan, 2004.

Stark, Rodney. *For the Glory of God: How Monotheism Led to Reformations, Science, Witch-Hunts, and the End of Slavery*. Princeton: Princeton University Press, 2003.

_____. *The Victory of Reason: How Christianity Led to Freedom, Capitalism, and Western Success*. New York: Random House, 2005.

Woods, Thomas E. *How The Catholic Church Built Western Civilization*. Washington, DC: Regnery, 2005.

CONCLUSION

Adam S. Francisco

The preceding essays have all illustrated different aspects of today's apologetic task. Responses to contemporary challenges such as the ones taken up in this volume (and conceivably many more) are vital to the promotion of the Christian faith as it falls under persistent attacks from opposing worldviews, religions, and a secularized and increasingly hostile culture. First Peter 3:15 enjoins us to engage in the enterprise. For these reasons—our contemporary environment and, more importantly, the scriptures themselves—Lutheran theologian David Scaer has described the whole endeavor as both necessary and biblical.[1] And make no mistake, while it may require "ingenuity, skill and rhetorical sensibility" and "appears to place undue weight on logic and rhetoric, it is serious theological business."[2] Not only does it expose the weakness of other worldviews, it works to establish a firm footing from which the Christian faith is confessed before the unbelieving world.

---

[1] See David P. Scaer, "Apologetics as Theological Discipline: Reflections on a Necessary and Biblical Task," in *Let Christ be Christ: Theology, Ethics, and World Religions in the Two Kingdoms*, ed. Daniel N. Harmelink (Huntington Beach: Tentatio Press, 1999), 299–307. Also see, John Warwick Montgomery, "Apologetics for the Twenty-first Century," in *Reasons for Faith: Making a Case for the Christian Faith*, ed. Norman Geisler and Chad V. Meister (Wheaton: Crossway, 2007), 41–52.

[2] William A. Dembski, "The Task of Apologetics," in *Unapologetic Apologetics: Meeting the Challenge of Theological Studies*, ed., William A. Dembski and Jay Wesley Richards (Downers Grove, IL: InterVarsity, 2001), 43.

There are those who would challenge this. In addition to the peculiarly Lutheran objections addressed in the introduction, the latest trend in theological discourse, as exemplified in many of the essays found, for example, in *Christian Apologetics in the Postmodern World,* suggests that such ventures are "no longer ... worth pursuing."[3] We live in an environment where no one is interested in what is true; thus, the argument goes, "Christians need not continue to answer 'the truth question.' "[4] Instead, we need only clarify and affirm who we are as a distinct people. "The church has a word to speak to the world not because it has a message that is objectively true," surmises Philip Kenneson; "Rather, the church has a word to speak to the world because it embodies an alternative politics, an alternative way of ordering human life made possible by Jesus Christ."[5]

Others have made similar cases. Dennis Hollinger, for example, argues that Christians in the postmodern world should "understand the church itself—a visible, corporate expression of the Christian worldview—to be an apologetic."[6] He argues for what James K. A. Smith describes as a "new apologetic," one that does not interact with unbelief and take seriously the criticisms of Christianity but rather one where the church starts to take itself and its life together more seriously. This, in itself, is not a bad recommendation; but it certainly is not an apologetic in the biblical (or historical) sense. Moreover, such a focus seems overly inward, directing Christians almost

---

[3] Philip D. Kenneson, "There's No Such Thing as Objective Truth, and It's a Good Thing, Too," in *Christian Apologetics in the Postmodern World,* ed. Timothy R. Philips and Dennis L. Okholm (Downers Grove, IL: InterVarsity, 1995), 160.

[4] Kenneson, "There's No Such Thing as Objective Truth," 161.

[5] Kenneson, "There's No Such Thing as Objective Truth," 162–63.

[6] Dennis Hollinger, "The Church as Apologetic: A Sociology of Knowledge Perspective," in *Christian Apologetics in the Postmodern World,* 183–93.

exclusively towards their "community's way of life" away from the unbelieving world.[7]

Now of course the church should be distinct. It is, after all, comprised of people who have been set apart by the Gospel. But— without even mentioning that these same holy people of God remain *simul justus et peccator*—one need only to look around and see that there are a wide variety of communities with peculiar ways of life that offer an alternative polity. Think of Islam and its comprehensive view of religion, politics, law, and morality. Or consider the allure of the cultural progressivism offered by the new atheists. And the list could go on. Not only do these communities offer different identities, though. They all purport to speak for the truth and, sometimes implicitly but oftentimes explicitly, denounce Christianity as a not so cleverly devised myth or just some story Christians continue to tell themselves for existential comfort. To shrink from apologetics in this environment is suicidal and, as J. P. Moreland puts it, a betrayal of the Gospel. The postmodern rejection of apologetics,

> is a form of intellectual pacifism that, at the end of the day, recommends backgammon while the barbarians are at the gate. It is the easy cowardly way out that removes the pressure to engage alternative conceptual schemes, to be different, to risk ridicule, to take a stand outside the gate. But it is precisely as disciples of Christ, even more, as officers in his army, that the pacifist way out is simply not an option. However comforting it may be, postmodernism is the cure that kills the patient, the military strategy that concedes defeat before the first shot is fired, the ideology that undermines its own claims to allegiance. And it is an immoral, coward's way out that is not worthy of a movement born out of the martyr's blood.[8]

---

[7] James K. A. Smith, *Who's Afraid of Postmodernism? Taking Derrida, Lyotard, and Foucault to Church* (Grand Rapids: Baker, 2006), 28–29.

[8] J. P. Moreland, "Postmodernism and Truth," in *Reasons for Faith*, 126.

Hopefully this volume will provide some small impetus for a recovery of or renewed emphasis on engaging those who have rejected the Christian faith, with the goal of persuading them that their doubts or objections to the Gospel are unfounded. The task is rarely easy. It often requires study and experience as well as patience, humility, and respect. But such is and always has been the life of those Paul calls ambassadors of Christ in contexts such as ours (2 Corinthians 5:20). Nevertheless, it was in such contexts—when it was customary for Paul (and the Early Church) to engage unbelief, even on its own turf (such as in the synagogue or even on Mars Hill), that the proclamation and defense of the Gospel turned the world upside down (Acts 17:6).

SCRIPTURE INDEX

CONTRIBUTORS

JOHN BOMBARO (M.Th., University of Edinburgh; Ph.D., University of London) is the pastor of Grace Evangelical Lutheran Church, San Diego, and Lecturer in the Theology and Religious Studies Department at the University of San Diego. He has regularly contributed essays to such publications as *The Clarion Review* and *Modern Reformation*, for which he also serves as an editorial advisor.

ADAM FRANCISCO (M.A., Concordia University, Irvine; D.Phil., University of Oxford) is Associate Professor of History at Concordia University, Irvine. He is the author of *Martin Luther and Islam* (2007), co-editor of *Theologia et Apologia: Essays in Reformation Theology and Its Defense* (2007), and a frequently sought speaker on the subjects of Islam and apologetics.

KOREY MAAS (M.Div., Concordia Seminary; D.Phil., University of Oxford) is Assistant Professor of History at Hillsdale College, Hillsdale, Michigan. He is the author of *The Reformation and Robert Barnes* (2010), co-editor of *Theologia et Apologia: Essays in Reformation Theology and Its Defense* (2007), and a regular contributor to both academic and popular periodicals.

ANGUS MENUGE (M.A. and Ph.D., University of Wisconsin, Madison) is Professor of Philosophy at Concordia University, Wisconsin. In addition to dozens of scholarly articles and reviews, he is the author of *Agents Under Fire: Materialism and the Rationality of Science* (2004), and editor of *Reading God's World: The Scientific*

Vocation (2004) and *Christ and Culture in Dialogue: Constructive Themes and Practical Applications* (1999).

JOSHUA PAGÁN (M. Div. and Ph.D., Concordia Theological Seminary) is Continuing Lecturer at Aboite Lutheran Church, Fort Wayne, Indiana. He has published in theological periodicals such as *Logia*, and regularly speaks in congregations and institutions of higher education on the topics of worldview and religious philosophy.

CRAIG PARTON (M.A., Simon Greenleaf School of Law; J.D., Hastings College of Law) is a trial lawyer and partner in the firm of Price, Postel, and Parma of Santa Barbara, California, and the American Director of the International Academy of Apologetics, Evangelism, and Human Rights. In addition to numerous articles and essays, he is the author of *Religion on Trial* (2008) and *The Defense Never Rests: A Lawyer's Quest for the Gospel* (2003).

MARK A. PIERSON (M.A., Concordia University, Irvine; M.Div., Concordia Theological Seminary) is Adjunct Professor of Theology and Philosophy at Concordia University, Irvine, and is currently pursuing a Ph.D. in New Testament Studies at Fuller Theological Seminary. His published essays have appeared in *Learning at the Foot of the Cross* (2010) and *Theologia et Apologia: Essays in Reformation Theology and Its Defense* (2007), as well as periodicals such as *Modern Reformation* and *For the Life of the World*.

Peer Reviewed

Concordia Publishing House

Similar to the peer review or "refereed" process used to publish professional and academic journals, the Peer Review process is designed to enable authors to publish book manuscripts through Concordia Publishing House. The Peer Review process is well-suited for smaller projects and textbook publication.

We aim to provide quality resources for congregations, church workers, seminaries, universities, and colleges. Our books are faithful to the Holy Scriptures and the Lutheran Confessions, promoting the rich theological heritage of the historic, creedal Church. Concordia Publishing House (CPH) is the publishing arm of The Lutheran Church—Missouri Synod. We develop, produce, and distribute (1) resources that support pastoral and congregational ministry, and (2) scholarly and professional books in exegetical, historical, dogmatic, and practical theology.

For more information, visit:
www.cph.org/PeerReview.

The American Muhammad

Joseph Smith, Founder of Mormonism

Alvin J. Schmidt

"At a time when Christianity is under assault worldwide, this painstakingly researched and superbly written account of seventy parallels between the founders of two thriving socio-political faiths, Islam and Mormonism, should be compulsory reading for all." —Uwe Siemon-Netto, Center for Lutheran Theology & Public Life

Alvin Schmidt has undertaken the challenging but informative task of documenting, discussing, and analyzing over seventy parallels that exist between Joseph Smith Jr. and Muhammad. He cites valid arguments why parallels between noteworthy individuals in history need to be studied in order to understand why they engaged in similar acts that left major marks in history. This fascinating book provides many facts not commonly known about Joseph Smith and Muhammad and will help readers see and understand how the teachings of these two men contradict biblical Christianity. (P) 296 pages. Paperback.

53-1199LBR   **978-0-7586-4029-1**

I Am Not Afraid: Demon Possession and Spiritual Warfare

True Accounts from the Lutheran Church of Madagascar

Robert H. Bennett

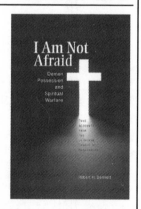

"I found this book too fascinating to put down. This timely work will be of interest not just to Lutherans . . . [but] to readers interested in the global church, in current views about demonology, and in Reformation views and especially historic Lutheran views about demonology." —Craig S. Keener, Asbury Theological Seminary

I Am Not Afraid is Rev. Dr. Robert Bennett's fascinating first-hand account of the spiritual warfare found within the Lutheran Church of Madagascar. Is spiritual warfare something new to the Church? Bennett reviews what the Bible, Church Fathers, and contemporary Lutheran leaders have to say. (P) 240 pages. Paperback.

53-1204LBR   **978-0-7586-4198-4**

www.cph.org • 1-800-325-3040

Concordia
Publishing House

Walther's Hymnal

Church Hymnbook for Evangelical Lutheran
Congregations of the Unaltered Augsburg Confession

Translated and Edited by Matthew Carver

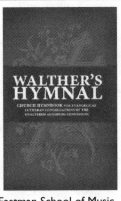

"*Walther's Hymnal* will serve not only as a rich devotional resource for our time but also as an impetus for future hymn writers as they add to our rich heritage."
—Rev. Dr. Paul Grime, Concordia Theological Seminary

"Matthew Carver's masterful translation of C. F. W. Walther's 1847 collection of German-language hymns opens a window on the mid-nineteenth-century revival of confessional Lutheranism in America." —Dr. Daniel Zager, Eastman School of Music

Now presented for the first time in English, *Walther's Hymnal* is an invaluable resource for history enthusiasts, church musicians, and anyone who wants insight into how our grandfathers sang and prayed. This is a chance to share in that song and prayer of the saints gone before us.

(P) 464 pages. Paperback.

53-1200LBR   **978-0-7586-4117-5**

Divine Kingdom, Holy Order

The Political Writings of Martin Luther

Jarrett A. Carty

"Carty has wisely selected and intelligently abridged Luther's most important political writings from 1520 to 1546. His introductions to the selections are careful and insightful, written with a full awareness of the large secondary literature. . . . A highly recommended resource."
—Denis R. Janz, Loyola University New Orleans

The canon of western political theory has long misrepresented Luther's political thought, mistaking it as a forerunner of the "freedom of conscience" or the "separation of church and state," or an ancestor of modern absolutism and even German totalitarianism. These misleading interpretations neglect Luther's central point: temporal government is a gift from God, worthy of honor and respect, independent yet complementary to the purpose and mission of the Church. Spanning Luther's career as a reformer, the writings in this anthology will demonstrate his resolve to restore temporal government to its proper place of honor and divine purpose. (P) 544 pages. Hardback.

53-1183LBR   **978-0-7586-2711-7**

When Was Jesus Really Born?

Early Christianity, the Calendar, and the Life of Jesus

Steven L. Ware

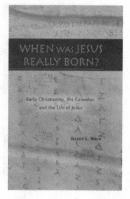

"Weaving scientific and historical scholarship with theological and pastoral concern, Dr. Ware's book provides a fresh, rigorous, and engaging new approach to an old issue. . . . This book deserves to be widely read by students and scholars, and by pastors and others exploring their faith."
—Andrew McGowan, The University of Melbourne

When was Jesus born? When did he die and rise from the grave? What does the timing of these events have to do with Christian theology and practice for the last 2,000 years? *When Was Jesus Really Born?* explores the issues faced by early Christians as they sought to proclaim and celebrate the most important events in human history—the birth, life, death, and resurrection of Jesus Christ. Includes illustrations, appendices, glossary, bibliography, and comprehensive indices of Scripture, dates, and subjects.

(P) 304 pages. Hardback.

53-1203LBR   **978-0-7586-4197-7**

Prepare the Way of the Lord

An Introduction to the Old Testament

R. Reed Lessing and Andrew E. Steinmann

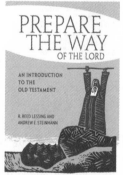

"This book will take you on a life-changing expedition through the Book of books. Your guides are as faithful as they are courageous, and you will not regret your time on this excursion with these authors." —James M. Hamilton, The Southern Baptist Theological Seminary

This new isagogics textbook examines and explores each book of the Old Testament, preparing students of the Bible to read Israel's texts with understanding and insight. It helps answer questions such as "What is helpful and what is detrimental to evangelical faith?" and "How do conservative scholars respond to critical views of the Old Testament?" The book interacts with scholars in a respectful way while providing evangelical assessments that foster historical and theological confidence in the Old Testament. (P) 580 pages. Hardback.

53-1187LBR   **978-0-7586-2832-9**

---

www.cph.org • 1-800-325-3040

Concordia
Publishing House